Neil Suggett is far more than a passionate and dedicate advocate of coaching. His writing is clear, warm and encouraging and the practical nature of his ideas are ready-made for anyone who shares his positive mind-set and his overriding optimism. Having used Neil's work in London, Brazil, South Korea and Bangkok, the reaction has always been the same: Yes, Yes, Yes! (And More! More! More!)

Adrian Ingham, International Leadership Development Consultant

I have been using his materials in Brazil in leadership courses which have been very well received.

This programme provides an excellent opportunity to use coaching approaches in our lives. I felt privileged to have Neil as my coach.

Magali do Nascimento de Paula, Education Consultant, Brazil

Neil was instrumental in designing, participating and developing a Management course for General Practitioners and their Practice Managers initially...his particular engaging, facilitative and skilful approach has proved invaluable to these groups as they often struggled over the years to adapt in a rapidly changing health care environment.

Neil's input has been fundamental...[in] a number of other educational initiatives and projects for General Practitioners. His coaching skills have enabled participants to reflect on their progress and make effective changes to benefit those they are supporting.

Dr Brynmor Neal, Provost, Thames Valley Faculty, Royal College of General Practitioners

His input has made me a better leader.

James Heale, Executive Head Teacher, Vyners Learning Trust

I have been fortunate to work with Neil over the last seven years. Neil's vast practical experience provides a deep and grounded resource which I have found invaluable.

Paul Thomas, Pastor,
King's Church, Amersham

Coaching is an essential part of any school leader's support network...Neil's skill as a coach facilitated new and creative solutions to what previously seemed insurmountable challenges.

John Ayres OBE, Executive Principal,
Eden Academy Trust

I cannot recommend him highly enough.

Leonora Prewett, Head Teacher,
Dunstable Icknield Lower School

I was so impressed with his work that I have asked him to coach my senior leadership team this year.

Robert Jones, Head Teacher,
Haydon School

On completion of [Neil's] session, I felt mentally rejuvenated...I was able to find clarity, understanding and focus on key professional development [issues] that have benefitted me since.

Executives in Oasis Learning Trust

Coaching has been a fantastic experience for me because of the skills of my coach - Dr Neil Suggett.

Debra Barlow, Head Teacher,
Hayes Park School

At the end of each coaching session, I always feel clearer and more confident...Neil brings a wealth of personal experience to the sessions.

Angela Doherty, Principal Adviser,
London Borough of Ealing

[Neil] offers support and trust to help me find my own outcomes to major challenges and issues.

Dorothy Chappell, Head Teacher,
Field End Infant School

LIVING
A
COACHING
LIFESTYLE

How to reach your potential in
30 bite-sized steps

Dr Neil Suggett CBE

laclguru.com

To Judith

My best friend, life-long coach and wife

With thanks to:

Adrian and Chris — for their support and encouragement

My colleagues and pupils at Hayes Park — 'the coaching school'

My Platinum Coaching Group — clients and friends

Stephen McClelland — my mentor who made this book a reality

Dr Neil Suggett CBE

Dr Neil Suggett is an acknowledged international authority on coaching and leadership development and a frequent speaker at major conferences.

Neil has worked as a teacher, head teacher, inspector and leadership coach. He has been a researcher at the National College, a Visiting Fellow at the Institute of Education and a Visiting Lecturer at Loughborough University and Brunel University. As one of the first National Leaders of Education Authority, he has worked extensively in people development and school improvement.

He has coached on five continents and is very passionate about the power of coaching to transform both individuals and organizations everywhere. His current 'Platinum Group' of coaching clients include senior leaders in all phases of education and senior church leaders.

In 2010, Neil was awarded the CBE in recognition of his services to education at home and abroad. In 2016, he was also honoured by The Royal College of General Practitioners in recognition of his services to medical education.

He now enjoys working as a leadership coach, coach trainer and writer. Currently, he is engaged in designing and delivering coach development programmes in a variety of contexts — locally, nationally and internationally. Most importantly, he is an ardent life-long learner committed to 'living a coaching lifestyle'.

Contents

Introduction: **How to use this book**
9

LS1 Where are you now?
17

LS2 What are your current goals?
23

LS3 What do you believe about your own potential?
29

LS4 How can you release more of your true potential?
35

LS5 Can you use a simple model to live a coaching lifestyle?
41

LS6 Are you setting the agenda for your own life?
47

LS7 What is your current reality?
53

LS8 What best options exist for your life's next phase?
59

LS9 Can you translate your goals into concrete action?
65

LS10 What have you learned in studying Module 1?
71

LS11 What is a coaching lifestyle?
77

LS12 How good is your listening?
83

LS13 What is the quality of the questions you are posing?
89

LS14 Can you transform plans into action?
95

LS15 Who provides you with support and challenge?
101

LS16 Are you committed to developing a coaching lifestyle?
107

LS17 What core values support your life's vision?
113

LS18 What should you say when you talk to yourself?
119

LS19 How good are you at managing yourself?
127

LS20 What have you learned in studying Module 2?
133

LS21 What is applied coaching?
141

LS22 Can I utilise a coaching approach at work?
149

LS23 Can coaching impact the organisational atmosphere?
157

LS24 Can coaching make people really matter at work?
163

LS25 Can coaching facilitate happiness-centred business?
169

LS26 Can coaching nurture relentless optimism?
177

LS27 Can coaching improve friendships?
183

LS28 Can coaching boost your most important relationships?
191

LS29 What is your definition of living a coaching lifestyle?
199

LS30 What next?
205

Endnote references
213

Quotation sources
214

Further reading
215

Index
217

INTRODUCTION

How to use this book

Notes

Introduction:
How to use this book

It seems that every life-form on this planet strives towards its maximum potential... except human beings. A tree does not grow to half its potential size and then say, 'I guess that will do.' A tree will drive its roots as deep as possible. It will soak up as much nourishment as it can, stretch as high and wide as nature will allow, and then look down as if to remind us of how much each of us could become if we would only do all we can. (Jim Rohn — American entrepreneur, author and motivational speaker)

Welcome to **living a coaching lifestyle** — LaCL for short. I hope you will reap a rich reward from your investment in this programme. Change is a constant in our lives. My intention is to provide you with the means to embrace constant change and to 'stretch as high and wide' as you choose.

My reasons for developing this programme are summarized in these four objectives.

> » To introduce you to the core skills of coaching.
>
> » To provide you with opportunities to develop these coaching skills, both for your own good and for the good of others.
>
> » To encourage you to enjoy change at home and at work.
>
> » To consider living a coaching lifestyle.

I began my formal coaching journey in 2002 by attending an award-bearing programme. This was the start of an evangelical passion in the power of coaching. At first I sought to apply coaching principles and philosophies at work and then it slowly dawned on me that it was equally as important to apply them at home. In this way, living a coaching lifestyle was born. I hope you will take the skills and ways of thinking embedded in this programme and make them your own.

Coaching is simply a way of helping people maximise their full potential. In its purest form, it is non-directive, non-judgemental and client-centred. The function of the coach is to:

» listen with compassion and sincerity

» question skilfully to clarify and deepen the thinking of the client

» promote clarity concerning the client's chosen action

» provide appropriate support and challenge at the right moment.

At a surface level, coaching is a series of tried and tested skills applied in a systematic way. At a deeper level, it is a performing art, demonstrated by a committed practitioner. The purpose of coaching is to help people grow. This resonates with my profound belief in the capacity of people to develop and blossom, myself included. Coaching is the perfect vehicle to enable people to embrace what they want to do and who they want to be.

My professional curriculum vitae can be summarised as a series of roles: teacher, head teacher, inspector, leadership developer and now coach. My personal life can be described in a similarly reductionist fashion: son, husband, father and now grandfather. This is clearly a false dichotomy as one set of roles impacts upon and is impacted by the other. Interestingly, a strong recurring theme across all these roles and my most ambitious definition of myself is 'learner'.

In Jim Rohn's terminology, I want to be the biggest tree I can be, with deep roots soaking up vital nourishment . I believe a coaching lifestyle enables you to grow and flourish, regardless of your age or stage in life. As a thought starter, I have conceptualised the five stages of my life in the table opposite (Table 1).

For me, Stage 1 revolved around family and education. I have vivid memories of sporting events, both playing in some and watching others. Examinations also loom large as transition points.

Stage 2 was about marriage, parenthood and increasing levels of responsibility in the workplace. It was also about spiritual awakening and exploring my faith.

My parents died during Stage 3 and I began to realise no one is immortal. My children grew up and left home and this stage was characterised by constant change. My pro-

Stage 1	0-20 years	Rapid physical and mental growth
Stage 2	20-40 years	Early career and early family stage
Stage 3	41-60 years	Maturing career and maturing parent stage
Stage 4	61-80 years	Opportunity zone and clarifying stage
Stage 5	81-100 years	Inner world and final preparation stage

Table 1 Stages of Life

fessional life also changed and developed and I discovered more about what I actually wanted to do.

I am now in Stage 4 and seeking to grasp the opportunities that are available. Being clear about my priorities is the basis of my time allocation. Faith, family and then work — clarity about who I am and what I want to do.

I am enjoying the fourth stage enormously and I want to help you get the most out of your current stage, whichever one that is. A coaching lifestyle involves developing an open-minded, questioning approach to all areas of your existence, at home, at work and at play. The material you will be presented with will enable you to identify where you are now and where you would like to go next. The format is designed to help you reflect on the past, plan for the future and, most importantly, make the most of the present.

The living a coaching lifestyle programme consists of thirty bite-sized chunks of material. These thirty learning steps have been divided into three modules, each containing ten learning steps. The three modules are structured in the following way:

Module 1: Designing the plans — employing the GROW model

Module 2: Laying the foundations — developing the core skills

Module 3: Building a coaching lifestyle — applying your learning

Each learning step builds on the previous ones. In this

way, a staircase is being constructed to support and challenge your thinking. The format of each learning step is the same: a starter question, a quotation, some explanatory text and the personal investment opportunity (the practical bit). Lastly, the learning step is summarised as a tweet of no more than 140 characters.

Your part of the deal is:

» to find your own answers to the **starter question**

» to reflect on the **quotation**

» to engage with the **explanatory text**

» to undertake the **personal investment opportunity**

I suggest you start a new learning journal to chart the development of your thinking and record your progress as you climb the staircase. Pace the material in whatever way works best for you. The journal should become your special friend, a place where you record your hopes and fears. It will tell its own story in due course.

To Do

Personal investment opportunity

This is the action bit, a chance to reflect and to plan. It is an investment in your personal development. Three things to think about...

* Decide the format of your learning journal — a file on your computer, a loose-leaf folder or an attractive hard-backed book — the choice is yours. Don't put off, start today.

* Jot down your hopes and fears for the programme and anything else you want to record before you embark upon the thirty learning steps. "Carpe diem"! Seize the day.

* When in doubt take every opportunity to live a coaching lifestyle, take a risk, try something new and record your reflections in your learning journal.

The days are long, but time is short — it seems one out of one dies! Make the most of your precious life, starting today. *Living a coaching lifestyle* is designed to help you realise your true potential — to achieve the happiness and success you seek. Now is the time for you to exercise your get-up-and-go and if you don't feel you have any, then fake it till you do!

To remember

> **Name** ✓
> @Username
>
> **Maximise your full potential by living a coaching lifestyle (LaCL) - the approach encompasses both work and home.**
>
> 21 Mar 2016

The introduction as a tweet

Notes

Where are you now?

LS1 is designed to help you:

* identify your starting point for LaCL

* reflect on who you are and what you do

* decide on your way of processing the materials

* start climbing the staircase

LIVING
A
COACHING
LIFESTYLE

Module 1

Module 1: Designing the plans — employing the GROW model

LS10 What have you learned in studying Module 1?

LS9 Can you translate your goals into concrete action?

LS8 What best options exist for your life's next phase?

LS7 What is your current reality?

LS6 Are you setting the agenda for your own life?

LS5 Can you use a simple model to live a coaching lifestyle?

LS4 How can you release more of your true potential?

LS2 What are your current goals?

LS3 What do you believe about your own potential?

LS1 Where are you now?

Where are you now?

A journey of a thousand miles begins with a single step. (Lao Tzu — ancient Chinese philosopher and writer)

The elevator to success is out of order. You'll have to use the stairs...one step at a time. (Joe Girard — 'the world's greatest salesman')

You have huge potential at every stage of your life. As I get older, I become more and more interested in the later stages! By engaging with this material you have begun to liberate the dormant power that lies within you. As the Lao Tzu quotation above asserts, a long journey starts with the decision to take the first step. Going up the stairs one step at a time will require effort and application, but the results are worth it. You are on the first step of this stairway to success, so let's start climbing!

The table of the stages of my life, as I have conceptualised them in the Introduction to the programme, is reproduced below (Table 2).

Stage 1	0-20 years	Rapid physical and mental growth
Stage 2	20-40 years	Early career and early family stage
Stage 3	41-60 years	Maturing career and maturing parent stage
Stage 4	61-80 years	Opportunity zone and clarifying stage
Stage 5	81-100 years	Inner world and final preparation stage

Table 2 Stages of Life

I have used the principles and practices of living a coaching lifestyle (LaCL) in a modified form with children and young adults and achieved great success. This book, however, is aimed at adults — Stages 2 to 5. You may wish to reconceptualise the stages of your life in a way that suits your thinking and your unique history. Ultimately, your current reality will have been shaped by the experiences you have had, the good ones and the not so good ones. Living a coaching lifestyle is designed to help you get the best out of today and the rest of your life. My plea is that you make the most of the Stage of Life you are in!

I have endeavoured to draw on my experiences as a coach, as a leadership developer and most importantly as a fellow learner, to structure this material in a coherent way. My mission is very ambitious: to support and challenge you to increase your level of satisfaction and enjoyment in who you are and what you do.

So let me ask you those two deceptively simple questions.

Who are you?

What do you do?

In later learning steps, I will differentiate between 'being' and 'doing' goals. For example, I enjoy being a husband, father, grandfather, sportsperson, coach and the list goes on. I do a wide variety of things, I earn money, cut the lawn, cook the dinner, write books and so on. When we meet new people they often ask us what we do in order to help them pigeon-hole us in their mental filing cabinet. I have yet to be asked who I am in the fullest sense!

This programme operates at both levels — being and doing. Many people ride Joe Girard's 'elevator of success' and when they get to the top discover they don't like the view or the reflection they see in the mirror. Use the stairs. Pause on each step and take time to have a good look around and look in the mirror. You may see things you have never seen before. You will be content with some of these things and others you may decide you choose to change.

Make a decision to take control of your life. You have choices about what you do and who you are. It feels very different when you say "I choose to do this" as opposed to "I have to do this". The first phrase puts you firmly in charge, while the second locates control elsewhere.

A coaching lifestyle is about embracing change. Traditional management of change models start with two basic questions:

A. Where are you now?

B. Where do you want to get to?

Question C is 'How do you get from A to B?' We have twenty-nine more opportunities for you to build a unique answer to this interesting question. As a starting point, I would like to invite you to engage with the personal investment opportunity set out below.

In order to get the most out of each personal investment opportunity, find a reflection strategy that works for you and fits your schedule. You may be a very systematic learner who likes to sit at a desk and make notes as you go. You may like to highlight parts of the text that particularly speak to you. Alternatively you may do your best thinking in the shower or driving your car. You may be a lark that operates best first thing in the morning or an owl who likes to burn the midnight oil. Do whatever works for you.

Whatever your style or preference, I urge you to record your thinking in a systematic and progressive way. Start your journal or folder, use your iPad or lap-top, or record your thoughts on your phone. Whatever method you choose, commit to living a coaching lifestyle starting today.

To do

Personal investment opportunity

* How do you conceptualise your current Stage of Life? Use my very simple model or design one of your own.

* How committed are you to getting the most from this stage of your life? Give yourself a score between 1 and 10, 1 is low and 10 is high.

Lao Tzu was writing in the sixth century BC, but the underlying principle is equally relevant today — every journey starts with a conscious decision, a first symbolic step.

Invest some protected time to reflect on how a coaching lifestyle might feel and look for you. Think about both 'being' and 'doing'.

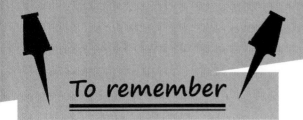

To remember

Name
@Username

Living a coaching lifestyle is about embracing change - take the first step. Develop a reflection strategy that works for you.

21 Mar 2016

LS1 as a tweet

LEARNING STEP 2

What are your current goals?

LS2 is designed to help you:

* see a future of limitless possibilities

* refine your 'doing' and 'being' goals

* take responsibility for your behavioural choices

* complete 'the wheel of life' exercise

Module 1 LS2

LIVING
A
COACHING
LIFESTYLE

Module 1

Module 1: Designing the plans — employing the GROW model

LS10 What have you learned in studying Module 1?

LS9 Can you translate your goals into concrete action?

LS8 What best options exist for your life's next phase?

LS7 What is your current reality?

LS6 Are you setting the agenda for your own life?

LS5 Can you use a simple model to live a coaching lifestyle?

LS4 How can you release more of your true potential?

LS2 What are your current goals?

LS3 What do you believe about your own potential?

LS1 Where are you now?

What are your current goals?

It is our choices that show what we truly are, far more than our abilities. (J K Rowling — British novelist, screenwriter and film producer)

Our personal and professional lives reflect the conscious and unconscious choices we have made in the past — no doubt some of these choices have proved to be very productive and some less so.

These decisions reflect our changing perception of our own abilities. Regardless of our history, our present and our future choices offer limitless possibilities. The world is our oyster, we can make radical new choices about the goals we want to pursue next.

National Life Tables 2010-12 (The Office for National Statistics) indicate that in England men will on average live to 83.3 years, while women will on average live to 85.9 years. You do the mathematics — you may live less or more than the national average, but either way life is finite and the clock is ticking. The days are long but the years are short — start living a coaching lifestyle (LaCL).

Reaching your true potential is about working out your 'being' and 'doing' goals and then having the courage to take the necessary action. 'Someday Isle' or rather 'Someday I'll' is not an attractive holiday destination, it is a classic manifestation of procrastination! Similarly defining yourself as a 'WASA', ('I was a .....') does not seem to be the most productive way of defining your present and future self.

Life is complex. We all wear many masks, and a myriad of people (parents, partners, children, friends, or colleagues) have expectations of who they want us to be. Some goals need to be negotiated with our nearest and dearest. In the final analysis, however, you decide by design or default who you want to be and what you want to do.

The *modus operandi* of **living a coaching lifestyle** is to increase your awareness of what is going on and to encourage you to take responsibility for your own behavioural choices. The responsibility for your present and future life rests with you. The most effective coaching is non-directive — you decide what you are going to do and enjoy the fruits of your choices. As your coach, I am blind to your world (I cannot see your reality), it is not my role to judge, but rather to support and challenge your thinking by asking you helpful questions. I will not tell you what

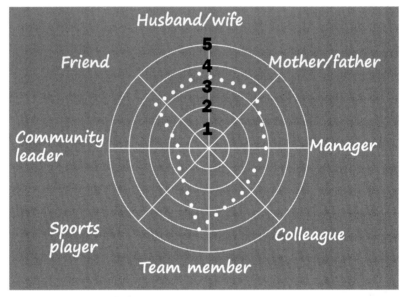

Figure 1 Example wheel of life

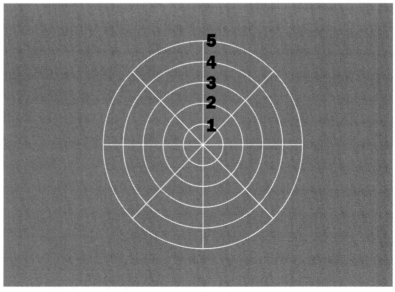

Figure 2 The wheel of life to complete

to do, because I cannot experience your reality or be presumptuous enough to pretend to know. You are the director of your own life. The learning steps are structured to encourage you to find your own answers.

You have enormous potential, you can choose how you want to grow and develop. Regardless of your chronological age and stage of life, your brain is capable of unimaginable development.

This programme is predicated upon you taking responsibility for your own learning and investing time and energy in your personal growth. The material is designed to put you in charge and you can be infinitely creative in the way you use it. All I ask is that you commit yourself to studying all thirty learning steps.

LS1 posed the question: *Where are you now?* The 'wheel of life' is an activity that helps you map this terrain in a bit more detail. Figure 1 opposite provides an example of one person's 'current reality'.

To Do

Personal investment opportunity

* Complete the wheel of life exercise and keep your 'current reality' wheel visible.

* Next consider your ideal score on each spoke. Plot your ideal score on the same wheel, but in a different colour. This is the 'future reality' you are aiming for.

* Identify three things you would like to do as a result of undertaking this exercise. These may be 'doing' goals (tasks to be achieved) or 'being' goals (how you want to be), or a combination of the two.

* J K Rowling suggests that our choices show who we really are. As a single mother with a young child, she chose to embark on a writing career, apparently with some success! What specific actions are you going to choose in order to realise your ideal 'future reality'?

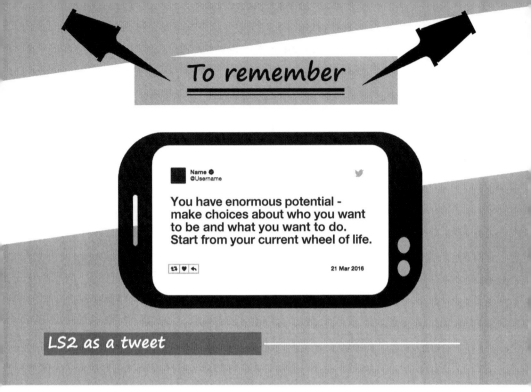

Start by identifying the six to eight spokes in your wheel of life that are important to you and record them on Figure 2. Reflect upon each spoke (area of your life) and allocate a score — 0 is the lowest possible score and 5 is the highest. Now draw a line between each spoke to make your 'current reality' wheel visible. What shape is your wheel? Which spokes are short and which ones are long? How do you feel about the shape?

I have completed this exercise on a number of occasions and used it with a large number of clients. A balanced life does not mean getting the same score on every spoke, but rather identifying the spokes where you would like to make changes in order to shift your current reality in that area of your life.

Inevitably you will have to make some difficult choices about where to focus both your time and your energy. Remember, if you continue to do what you have always done, inevitably you will get what you have always got! If you don't like something, change it!

LEARNING STEP 3

What do you believe about your own potential?

LS3 is designed to help you:

* verbalise your perception of your potential

* develop a questioning approach to life

* adopt an optimistic mindset

* make changes one step at a time

Module 1 LS3

LIVING
A
COACHING
LIFESTYLE

Module 1

Module 1: Designing the plans — employing the GROW model

LS10 What have you learned in studying Module 1?

LS9 Can you translate your goals into concrete action?

LS8 What best options exist for your life's next phase?

LS7 What is your current reality?

LS6 Are you setting the agenda for your own life?

LS5 Can you use a simple model to live a coaching lifestyle?

LS4 How can you release more of your true potential?

LS2 What are your current goals?

LS3 What do you believe about your own potential?

LS1 Where are you now?

What do you believe about your own potential?

We cannot teach people anything — we can only help them discover it within themselves. (Galileo — Italian astronomer, mathematician and philosopher)

The only constant in life is change. **Living a coaching lifestyle (LaCL)** focuses on future possibilities rather than dwelling on past mistakes. Your view of yourself will have been formed over your life so far. Your behaviour is a function of the experiences you have had — your personal history. You will have been told many things, by many people, about your true potential and you have to choose which voices you believe. The critical voices often sound louder! So I ask again, "What do you believe about your own potential?" The most significant voice is your own.

The wheel of life exercise encouraged you to identify the three spokes where you choose to make changes. Look at these three domains in a bit more detail and review and refine the goals you set. If you carry on doing what you have always done it is likely that you will keep getting the same result. (I will keep repeating this mantra until you take some notice!) A different outcome requires a different input — a change of some behaviours is needed. A coaching inner dialogue will help focus your behavioural choices by posing variations of the following questions:

Does my goal encapsulate what I really want to do or be?

Where am I now in relation to this goal?

What options have I got that will get me from where I am now to where I want to be?

How much time and energy am I prepared to invest in achieving this goal?

How will it be when I have achieved this goal?

People spend lots of money on puzzles — Sudoku, crosswords, computer games, the list is endless. Adopting a questioning approach to your personal and professional opportunities and challenges is an absorbing activity and it doesn't cost anything! The development of a coaching lifestyle will provide you with a priceless life-skill that can be deployed at critical moments, both now and in the future.

As Galileo identifies above, the challenge is to discover the resources and talents within yourself that you did not realise you possessed. You know more than you realise, but the trick is to be able to locate this knowledge at the most opportune moment. **Living a coaching lifestyle** starts from the premise that you have the answer already, you simply need help in uncovering it. That is why I am presenting this series of thirty learning steps to help you capitalise on your hidden potential.

I suggest (in a non-directive way) that you adopt an optimistic mindset and become your own cheerleader. This may feel slightly uncomfortable and unnatural, but please

To Do

Personal investment opportunity

* Which of your current behaviours are supporting a coaching lifestyle? Do more of this!

* What behaviours are hindering the achievement of your chosen goals? Eradicate or reduce these unproductive behaviours. It is not rocket science — just plain old common sense.

* Galileo played a major scientific role in the Renaissance and placed great emphasis upon self-discovery — the answers lie within us!

* Take another look at the three goals you identified in LS2 — do you want to review or redefine them in the light of this learning step?

* Invest in the three-step approach laid out above for each of your three goals. (write — visualise — feel)

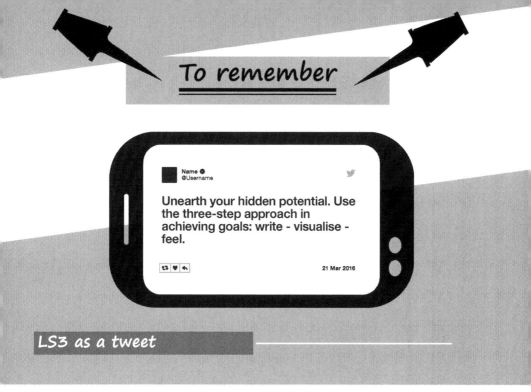

Name
@Username

Unearth your hidden potential. Use the three-step approach in achieving goals: write - visualise - feel.

21 Mar 2016

LS3 as a tweet

just humour me. Look at the three goals you identified in LS2 and imagine that you have reached your ideal outcome. Employ this three-step approach:

» Write a description of each ideal outcome in your journal.

» Close your eyes and visualise how the outcome will look and feel — if you can't visualise it go back and re-write the description.

» Simulate the feelings that you will experience when you achieve the goal.

Living a coaching lifestyle is designed to unlock your potential. Most self-development writers suggest we use less than 10% of our potential — that seems like a criminal waste. Give yourself the benefit of the doubt, resist negative-self-talk and replace it with an optimistic, questioning approach to life. Capture your successes and learning experiences in your learning journal, these are capital in your emotional bank account.

A coaching life style embraces both your interactions with others and your interactions with yourself. A good listener, who asks supportive and developmental questions, will always be popular and helpful to family, friends and

33

colleagues. This lifestyle starts on the inside. Listen to your own self-talk, ask yourself supportive and developmental questions and take the necessary action. Thus you are modelling the powerful impact of a coaching lifestyle. Your behaviours are far more eloquent than your words!

Look at the stairs in your house. Even if you are a gifted Olympic athlete, it is impossible to get from the bottom of the stairs to the top in one jump (notwithstanding wearing your underpants on the outside). It works much better to take one step at a time. This programme is a staircase with thirty steps. My hard-won personal experience is that change happens in the same way, one step at a time.

LEARNING STEP 4

How can you release more of your true potential?

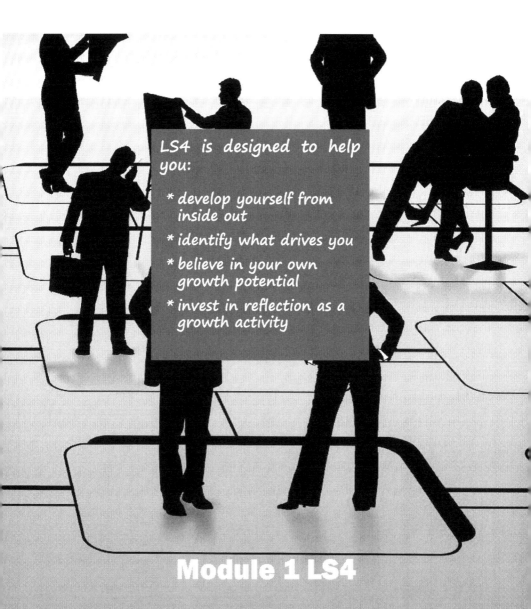

LS4 is designed to help you:

* develop yourself from inside out
* identify what drives you
* believe in your own growth potential
* invest in reflection as a growth activity

Module 1 LS4

LIVING
A
COACHING
LIFESTYLE

Module 1

LS10 What have you learned in studying Module 1?

LS9 Can you translate your goals into concrete action?

LS8 What best options exist for your life's next phase?

LS7 What is your current reality?

LS6 Are you setting the agenda for your own life?

LS5 Can you use a simple model to live a coaching lifestyle?

LS4 How can you release more of your true potential?

LS2 What are your current goals?

LS3 What do you believe about your own potential?

LS1 Where are you now?

How can you release more of your true potential?

Learning is about one's relationship with oneself and one's ability to exert the effort, self-control and critical self-assessment necessary to achieve the best possible results. (Linda B. Nilson — American academic, speaker and writer)

The holy grail of leadership success has proved elusive to me for more than thirty years. I have read libraries of books on the subject, attended a plethora of expensive seminars, listened to the finest speakers and still the relentless search goes on. Stop Press — I now know where to look! The title of Kevin Cashman's book provides a neon signpost, *Leadership from the inside out*. So that's what Galileo meant!

Looking inwards is a richly rewarding activity that produces significant dividends. Learning about your strengths and next areas of development is a never ending process. So where are you now? Record your special talents and the successes you have achieved in your learning journal. Try to be objective, look for evidence and seek feedback from people you trust. Understanding yourself is the precursor to understanding others. Your potential is unique — there is no other person who is exactly the same as you.

Work out what drives you, the nature of your aspirations and priorities. Planning a route becomes a lot easier when you know where you are going and where you are starting from. Personal authenticity involves being clear about who you are both at home and at work, rather than striving to be someone others expect you to be. Develop a lifestyle that fits who you are and that maximises your true potential.

Success in anything is in part built on faith. The starting point in releasing your true potential is to believe you have some! Take a leap of faith in yourself and behave in a self-confident way. The first person you have to convince is yourself. Resist the inner critic and practise positive self-talk. Bank positive feedback from people whose opinions you value. Reward the behaviours you want to reinforce, the behaviours that serve you. Reduce the behaviours that do not serve you, resist self-sabotage.

Reflection is a richly rewarding growth activity. The challenge is to find the time and space to reflect in the helter-skelter of daily living. The strategy that works for me is to sit with a favourite pen and a blank pad and see what arrives on the paper. Freshly ground coffee and background music add real value to the process. My best thinking is done first thing in the morning. Find your best time. Are you a lark or an owl? Do you wake raring to go or do you do your best thinking later in the day? Find out what fits your personal preferences and can be accommodated in your busy lifestyle.

Try to build a reflective thinking routine. The three Bs offer possible answers to where is the best place to reflect:

- » bed (the alpha state, between waking and sleeping)
- » bath (running water stimulates thinking)
- » bus (the journey provides dedicated time)

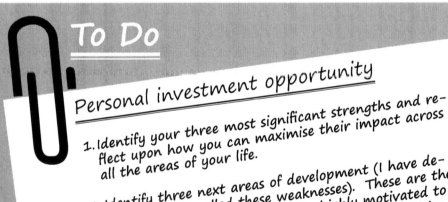

To Do

Personal investment opportunity

1. Identify your three most significant strengths and reflect upon how you can maximise their impact across all the areas of your life.

2. Identify three next areas of development (I have deliberately not called these weaknesses). These are the development areas that you are highly motivated to address and that you see as potential opportunities rather than insurmountable problems.

3. Develop a reflection strategy that works for you, make it a priority, build it into your schedule. This is a high-return investment!

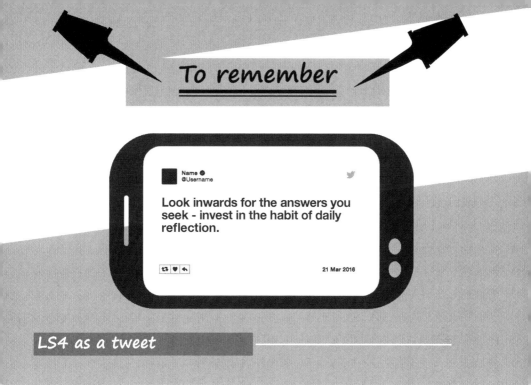

Name ●
@Username

Look inwards for the answers you seek - invest in the habit of daily reflection.

21 Mar 2016

LS4 as a tweet

A favourite arm-chair, the shower or your own car probably work just as well. Invest in developing a reflection routine that over time will become a habit. You will know that it is an enduring habit when you become unconsciously competent — you do it without thinking about it. Identify:

» the best time of day

» the best place or setting

» the best materials (pen, paper and coffee or iPad and/or red wine)

Linda B. Nilson was founding director of the Office for Teaching Effectiveness and Innovation at Clemson University. Her quotation above suggests one's relationship with oneself is at the heart of unleashing personal potential. All relationships require an investment of time and care and your relationship with yourself is no different. Indeed, the quality of your learning over the course of this programme will reflect your ability and willingness to exert effort, self-control and critical self-assessment.

We have a tendency to look outwards for miracle solutions when the real answers lie within!

Can you use a simple model to live a coaching lifestyle?

LS5 is designed to help you:

* balance 'doing' and 'being' goals
* understand the GROW model
* experiment with it at home and at work
* make the model your own

Module 1 LS5

LIVING
A
COACHING
LIFESTYLE

Module 1

LS10 What have you learned in studying Module 1?

LS9 Can you translate your goals into concrete action?

LS8 What best options exist for your life's next phase?

LS7 What is your current reality?

LS6 Are you setting the agenda for your own life?

LS5 Can you use a simple model to live a coaching lifestyle?

LS4 How can you release more of your true potential?

LS2 What are your current goals?

LS3 What do you believe about your own potential?

LS1 Where are you now?

Can you use a simple model to live a coaching lifestyle?

GROW captures a key aspect of what coaching is and does: enabling people to grow, to develop their capabilities, achieve high performance and gain fulfilment. (Graham Alexander — British innovator and leading edge thinker)

Living a coaching lifestyle is about both 'doing' and 'being'. Our education system and workplaces are usually characterised by 'doing' — passing examinations, achieving results, doing well, getting the job done. It feels very tiring and very competitive! The 'being' mode, by contrast, provides a different way of relating to the world. It is about the here and now, your experience of the present moment, how it feels to be you at this time.

As you live through different phases of your life the doing/being balance will shift and change. In the early stages of life, you may be very goal-orientated and later on you may be more interested in exploring your personal uniqueness. These two perspectives are not mutually exclusive, in fact quite the reverse, they are complementary. It is perfectly possible to focus on both what you want to do, your goals ('doing') and how you want to be, your character and lifestyle ('being'). The next four sessions of the programme are at first glance about introducing a structure for successful 'doing', but also provide an opportunity to reflect on how you are 'being' as you internalise the framework.

GROW is a simple and effective model that can be applied to a whole range of areas of your life. In their book *Supercoaching*[1], Graham Alexander and Ben Renshaw document the genesis of GROW. They had employed a variety of acronyms to try to capture the essence of the coaching process when they had an eureka moment and the GROW model was born.

Experiment with the model, use it at every available opportunity at home and at work. In this way the model will become a life-long friend. The power of the model resides

43

in its simplicity. There are other far more esoteric coaching models around, but why complicate life? Internalise the four stages, make it your own and if opportunities don't come naturally, create some artificial ones! As the golf legend Gary Player famously said "The more I practise, the luckier I get".

This slightly modified version of their original model has four clear stages, as depicted in Table 3 below.

| Defining the goal clearly is a major challenge in many areas of our busy lives (see LS2). What do I want to achieve by undertaking this course of action?

A well-formed goal has a galvanising effect as it draws you forward to an eagerly anticipated outcome. Goal-setting is a core life-skill, both for a successful professional life and for a fulfilling private existence.

Define a well-formed goal, set a clear time-scale and establish clear measures of success. Now you are up and running. | Your current reality identifies your starting point. It is the way you see the current state of play (see LS1).

This perception may be objectively accurate or simply your subjective version of reality, that reflects your current 'being'. In one sense it does not matter, feelings are influential facts and you start from what you believe to be true. Exploring your current reality provides an opportunity to examine your thinking at the conscious level. You may wish to triangulate your perceptions by seeking the opinion of someone you trust or by simply putting yourself in another person's shoes and seeing the issue through their eyes. |

Table 3 The GROW model

» G — goal

» R — current reality

» O — options

» W — will stage

The GROW model is a utilitarian vehicle, you choose how you want to drive it. You are at the wheel and the choice of driving style is yours!

We usually have far more options than we think — the challenge is to open your eyes wide enough to see them.

A resourceful search for options bears much fruit and provides us with choices. When we have a clear goal, the reticular activating system (RAS) opens up and searches out ways of achieving success. (More of the reticular activating system later in the programme.)

After the range of choices has been explored, it is then a judgement call about which is the best option.

The final section of the **GROW** model really adds significant power to living a coaching lifestyle.

How committed are you at the level of the will to taking the action? I find it very helpful to ask clients (and myself) scalar questions at this point. On a scale of 1 to 10, with 1 being low and 10 being high, how committed are you? The number chosen provides a window into the likely outcome. A low score suggests I can't be bothered to take the necessary action or I lack the confidence to try. A high score usually means I can't wait to get on with it! If you can't increase your score, go back and set a different goal that will engage you.

To Do

Personal investment opportunity

1. Reflect on the doing/being balance in your life at this time — do a 'brain dump' in your learning journal. Dump the first things that come into your head on the page and then pause and reflect upon them in a more considered fashion.

2. Graham Alexander is an innovator and leading edge thinker. Internalise the four stages of his GROW model and take opportunities at home and at work to test drive the model.

3. Record your review and reflections on one GROW session at home and one at work.

To remember

Name ●
@Username

GROW is a simple and effective model that can be used at work and at home - internalise it.

21 Mar 2016

LS5 as a tweet

Are you setting the agenda for your own life?

LS6 is designed to help you:

* set 'doing' and 'being' goals at home and at work

* capitalise on the power of your reticular activating system (RAS)

* use SMART models to set goals

* maximise left brain and right brain approaches

Module 1 LS6

LIVING
A
COACHING
LIFESTYLE

Module 1

Module 1: Designing the plans — employing the GROW model

LS10 What have you learned in studying Module 1?

LS9 Can you trans-late your goals into concrete action?

LS8 What best op-tions exist for your life's next phase?

LS7 What is your current reality?

LS6 Are you setting the agenda for your own life?

LS5 Can you use a simple model to live a coaching lifestyle?

LS4 How can you release more of your true potential?

LS2 What are your current goals?

LS3 What do you believe about your own potential?

LS1 Where are you now?

Are you setting the agenda for your own life?

Your goal should be just out of reach, but not out of sight. (Denis Waitley — American author, motivational speaker and consultant)

The first stage in the GROW model is to construct a well-formed goal. In both your personal and professional life, getting the goal right clarifies what you are trying to do. This gives the unconscious mind something to work with. When I have established my destination, I can get focussed on spotting the right signposts. My reticular activating system (RAS) is engaged and open for business.

The importance of defining a clear goal cannot be over-emphasised. Setting a clear goal is the launch pad for personal and corporate success and fulfilment. If you don't know where you are aiming, any outcome will do. Let's see what we hit and retrospectively call it the target! Follow the old artillery maxim — get ready, take aim and only then, fire.

S	specific
M	measurable
A	achievable
R	relevant
T	time-bound, time-related, trackable

Table 4 The SMART goal concept

Sometimes goals in a particular area of our life or work are a bit hazy and so a preliminary stage to goal setting could be required. TGROW advocates an exploration of **T**opic before we launch into goal setting. An exploration of a general topic can be the ancestor of a well-formed goal. Unravelling the general in order to arrive at the specific is akin to the warm-up before vigorous exercise:

What is currently on my mind?

Can I be more precise and make that more specific?

Am I ready to create a SMART goal?

SMART is a very widely used acronym in the management literature. Most people agree on the first four letters and there are a number of variations on the T (Table 4).

So as you embark upon a coaching dialogue establish a SMART goal. This is not a straight-jacket, but rather a general direction. Your goal will be clarified or modified, or even changed completely, as you work through the current reality stage. Nevertheless, a starting SMART goal provides a firm foundation upon which to build the coaching process and to inform the final plan of action.

Goal-setting is an empowering way of thinking about the future and galvanising yourself to turn this aspiration into a reality. Achieving an appropriate balance of 'doing' and 'being' goals reflects both your stage of life and your particular personal circumstances. A logical, left-brain approach lends itself to setting SMART 'doing' goals. The challenge is to liberate the richness and colour of the right brain to incubate 'being' goals.

'Being' goals can be slippery and hard to tie down because they are qualitative and based on feelings. How do you want to be? How do you want to feel? Work goals are usually quantitative, measurable and time-related, whereas life goals are softer, harder to measure and indefinite. In an attempt to provide balance, I have redefined the SMART acronym to address 'being' goals (Table 5).

Define for yourself what 'being' SMART means. Waitley suggests above that goals should be stretching and achievable. As a teacher, parent and grandparent, I have observed the power of a correctly calibrated goal. Set too

S	self-generated
M	meaningful to me
A	active
R	responsive to my changing circumstances
T	timely

Table 5 The SMART goal concept redefined for 'being' goals

To Do

Personal investment opportunity

Have another look at your 'Wheel of Life' (LS2). What progress are you making and do you want to refine any of those goals?

Dennis Waitley is an American motivational speaker and writer and is a passionate advocate of being optimistic about our achievement potential. Select one of your 'doing' goals to turn into a SMART, stretch target and select one of your 'being' goals for the alternative SMART treatment. Log these in your journal.

Reflect on the balance of 'doing' and 'being' in the goals you have set yourself both now and in the past.

To remember

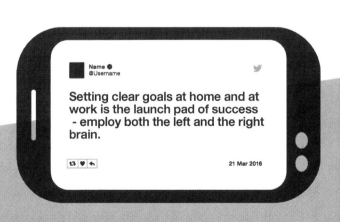

Name
@Username

Setting clear goals at home and at work is the launch pad of success - employ both the left and the right brain.

21 Mar 2016

LS6 as a tweet

high, a goal leads to disenchantment and disaffection. Set too low it leads to laziness and boredom. Set just right, it generates challenge and motivation.

Disperse the fog and clarify your 'doing' and 'being' goals. How will it look and feel when a particular goal is achieved? Invest in your goal-setting and clarify the outcomes you desire. High achievers in sport, employment and life set stretch goals. What are yours?

What is your current reality?

LS7 is designed to help you:

* define your current reality (CR)

* interrogate this CR in some detail

* have a coaching conversation with someone you trust

* remember to invest by staying longer in CR

Module 1 LS7

LIVING
A
COACHING
LIFESTYLE

Module 1

Module 1: Designing the plans – employing the GROW model

LS10 What have you learned in studying Module 1?

LS9 Can you translate your goals into concrete action?

LS8 What best options exist for your life's next phase?

LS7 What is your current reality?

LS6 Are you setting the agenda for your own life?

LS5 Can you use a simple model to live a coaching lifestyle?

LS4 How can you release more of your true potential?

LS2 What are your current goals?

LS3 What do you believe about your own potential?

LS1 Where are you now?

What is your current reality?

There are no facts, only interpretations. (Friedrich Nietzsche — German philosopher and philologist)

This learning step has been designed to provide an opportunity for you to draw aside from the busyness of your everyday existence and to take stock. LS5 focused upon your balance of 'doing' and 'being' goals. This may be a false dichotomy as we are 'being' while we are 'doing' and vice-versa. Making sense of our world is an interpretive process that provides us with the map and compass to realise our goals — it is our reality. Our reality may shift and be modified over time, but the starting point at any given time is our **current reality.**

Some years ago I worked with the coaches at a school in Australia. In an attempt to expedite the coaching process they decided to reduce the GROW model to the GOW model. In others words, they omitted the 'reality' stage and went straight from the goal to the options. This proved to be a significant mistake as it emaciated the whole process. The learning point was the importance of exploring 'current reality' in some detail. In fact, when in doubt stay longer in this stage!

Exploring current reality is an investment which will save you time in the options section. It is also an opportunity to double check that you have defined your goal correctly — identifying the real issue you are seeking to address. When you really **hear** yourself exploring the details of the situation you are describing, it may take on a different texture. In a slightly mysterious way, hearing yourself say something out loud can feel very different to simply thinking it.

The Nietzsche quotation suggests there are no facts, only our subjective interpretations of the reality around us. (This may be a very challenging proposition for some of you empirical scientists.) We see the world through the spectacles of our previous experiences and we are predisposed to certain interpretations. This is why it is so powerful to have a coaching conversation with a trusted other. The conversation provides us with the opportunity to check our perceptions. Skilful questioning takes us deeper and wider and ultimately provides us with more options.

The colleagues in Australia described above had a laudable desire to streamline the coaching experience. However, omitting the 'current reality' stage had the opposite effect — it impoverished the process by removing the foundation upon which the rest of the model is constructed. New coaches often rush through the reality stage in order to reduce their own anxiety by getting some options out on the table. This is almost always a mistake!

When in doubt stay longer in 'current reality', both when you are coaching yourself and when you are coaching other people. Effective coaching requires sustained reflection and an accurate assessment of where you are now. Exploring current reality generates embryonic options and facilitates a smooth transition into the next stage of the GROW model.

When you are coaching yourself you can record your current reality in your learning journal. Try reading it out loud and listen for insights and clues that will inform future action. Talk it through with a trusted other and encourage them to supportively challenge your reality in a non-judgemental way. Your presenting issue may not be the real issue and this will become apparent as the coaching dialogue develops.

The 4Fs model depicted and defined in Table 6 is an effective way to interrogate current reality.

F1	Facts: What evidence is available?
F2	Feelings: How does this make me feel?
F3	Findings: Can I use these facts and feelings as a springboard to action?
F4	Future: Where next?

Table 6 The 4F concept

We often treat our feelings as facts. These feelings provide the motivation and springboard for our actions. Now these feelings may be based on hard facts, for which some

To Do

Personal investment opportunity

The German philosopher Nietzsche's radical questioning of the objectivity of truth provides an interesting perspective in the current reality section of the GROW model.

Revisit the two goals you identified in LS6 and re-examine what 'truths' you noted in the current reality section.

Reflect on these truths and apply the 4Fs model.

Talk over your outcomes with a trusted other and hear how it sounds when you speak it out loud.

To remember

Name
@Username

Always explore the 'current reality' in detail - this stage needs to be accorded the time and energy it deserves.

21 Mar 2016

LS7 as a tweet

objective evidence exists, or they may be our subjective response to specific circumstances. Differentiating facts and feelings informs our data gathering and the findings help us to move forward on the future we are seeking to construct.

In summary, the current reality stage is a key part of the coaching process and it needs to be accorded the time and energy it deserves. Investing the time to explore your current reality is a high return activity that will expedite the options stage later.

What best options exist for your life's next phase?

LS8 is designed to help you:

* understand that options emerge naturally from CR

* see that LaCL encourages you to examine alternatives

* use both divergent and convergent thinking

* decide your best option and then take action

Module 1 LS8

LIVING
A
COACHING
LIFESTYLE

Module 1

LS10 What have you learned in studying Module 1?

LS9 Can you translate your goals into concrete action?

LS8 What best options exist for your life's next phase?

LS7 What is your current reality?

LS6 Are you setting the agenda for your own life?

LS5 Can you use a simple model to live a coaching lifestyle?

LS4 How can you release more of your true potential?

LS2 What are your current goals?

LS3 What do you believe about your own potential?

LS1 Where are you now?

Module 1: Designing the plans — employing the GROW model

What best options exist for your life's next phase?

We must dare to think 'unthinkable' thoughts. We must learn to explore all the options and possibilities that confront us in a complex and rapidly changing world. (William Fulbright — American senator and educator)

As we rehearsed in LS7, options often emerge from a thorough exploration of current reality. This current state of play provides a clear starting point from which we can begin to explore the possible ways forward. A coaching approach enables us to examine alternatives in a systematic way. We always have more options than we initially believe we have. A powerful opening gambit is to pose the question: *What would happen if I did nothing?* The answer to this question offers a glimpse of the level of commitment to taking some action!

Let's revisit an overview of a coaching approach and locate the process of generating and evaluating options within the whole GROW model.

G — What is my goal?

I want to have a clear statement of intent, with a compelling picture of the desired outcome that will motivate me to take the action required.

R — What is the current reality?

My perception of the current state of play provides the starting point for mapping the journey ahead. It also establishes the basis for generating a range of options about how best to proceed.

O — What options have I got?

The options section opens by generating possible ways to proceed. It then moves into an evaluation of each of the options in order to decide upon the most favourable path.

W — How committed am I to taking the action?

This is where the rubber hits the road to use a well-worn euphemism. Nothing will change unless I am prepared to invest energy and take action.

The first part of the options stage involves going as wide and deep as possible, divergent thinking in the fullest sense. Nothing should be ruled out at this point. We always have far more options than we think — the challenge is to open our eyes wide enough to see them. Day dreams, night dreams, reflection or humorous asides may bring options into play. Harvest all the options you can conceive and record them in a way that facilitates evaluation and comparison.

Having a clear goal, unleashes the reticular activating system to seek out possible ways forward. The RAS is an automatic goal seeking mechanism that works to help you achieve the goals you have established. Dr Maxwell Maltz in his classic book *Psycho-cybernetics*[1], published in 1960, identifies our automatic goal seeking 'servo- mechanism'. He doesn't use the words reticular activating system, but it is the same process. (Incidentally much of the modern self-help literature is based upon Maxwell Maltz's ideas published around 50 years ago.)

The challenge is to create a very specific picture of our goal

To Do

Personal investment opportunity

Make friends with your reticular activating system (RAS). James William Fulbright was a United States Senator committed to international educational exchanges (The Fulbright Program). His quote highlights the importance of generating and exploring options and possibilities. The RAS is there to help!

Choose two topics that you would like to focus on over the next week. One might be a 'doing' initiative and one might be a 'being' initiative. The choice is yours. Note them in your learning log and each day record what your RAS has come up with. Relax and see what appears.

in our conscious mind. The RAS will pass this on to our unconscious mind — which will then help us achieve the goal. It does this by bringing to our attention all the relevant information which otherwise might have remained as 'background noise'. The reason psycho-cybernetics is so significant is that the RAS will prevent our goal messages getting through to our unconscious if our self-image is not congruent with our goals.

Keeping the RAS open for business, generates a rich variety of options. The next part of the options section involves figuring out which is the best course of action by employing a convergent thinking approach. The process moves from one of suspending your judgement in the option generation phase to becoming evaluative about choosing the 'best' option. The selection process involves both thinking and feeling considerations. Indeed, it is a rich blend of evaluation and intuition. It is a combination of systematic thinking and performance art.

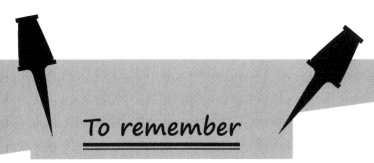

To remember

Name
@Username

Keep the RAS open for business and you will find you have more options that you thought - choose by combining evaluation and intuition.

21 Mar 2016

LS8 as a tweet

A quotation ascribed to Albert Einstein sums it up brilliantly: "The rational mind is a faithful servant; the intuitive mind a sacred gift. The paradox of modern life is that we have begun to worship the servant and defile the Divine."

The chosen option can be turned into a viable action plan in the will section. Once a decision has been made it is easier to add detail about the way in which it will be achieved. Resist the temptation to engage in endless analysis that leads to paralysis rather than action. Decide upon your best option and go for it.

Can you translate your goals into concrete action?

LS9 is designed to help you:

* comprehend the power of the will

* use scalar questions to ascertain the level of commitment

* translate thinking into concrete action plans

* seek both support and challenge

Module 1 LS9

LIVING A COACHING LIFESTYLE

Module 1

LS10 What have you learned in studying Module 1?

LS9 Can you translate your goals into concrete action?

LS8 What best options exist for your life's next phase?

LS7 What is your current reality?

LS6 Are you setting the agenda for your own life?

LS5 Can you use a simple model to live a coaching lifestyle?

LS4 How can you release more of your true potential?

LS2 What are your current goals?

LS3 What do you believe about your own potential?

LS1 Where are you now?

Module 1: Designing the plans — employing the GROW model

Can you translate your goals into concrete action?

> What distinguishes a successful person from others is not their strength, not their knowledge, but rather their will. (Jason Vale — author, motivational speaker and lifestyle coach)

I choose to identify the fourth part of the GROW model as the **will** stage. Other people have variously described it as the 'wrap-up' or the 'work' stage. Regardless of the name, it is where the action is planned. My preference for calling it the **will** stage is because your commitment at the level of your will is the key determinant of success!

Scalar questions are helpful in terms of ascertaining our true level of commitment. Ask yourself the following question in relation to any goal you are setting:

> "On a scale of 1 to 10, with 1 being low and 10 being high, how committed am I to taking the necessary action to achieve this goal?"

Scores below seven suggest a lack of real commitment to the action. "I would like the desired outcome but I am too unsure or too lazy to take the action necessary to make it happen." Remember if you always do what you have always done, you will always get what you have always got. Doing the same thing and expecting a different outcome is the triumph of hope over reality. A different outcome requires a change of behaviour. This is where your commitment at the level of the will really comes into play.

Scores of 7, 8, or 9 beg the question:

> "What do I need to do to increase my level of commitment from a 7 to an 8, (8 to 9 and so on)?"

There is no magic in the numbers themselves — this is simply a method of calibrating your perception of your level of commitment to achieving the desired outcome. A score of 10 indicates that you are totally committed and ready to translate this momentum into a clear plan of action.

Jason Vale suggests in the above quote that **will** is the key to success. In order to generate the required level of will-power we may need support or challenge, or a combination of the two. It is worth reviewing your 'mastermind group' and asking yourself who can I ask for the support or challenge I need to increase my level of commitment. Your 'mastermind group' can be made up of living people you interact with or a virtual group of gurus and fictional characters you have accessed through their writings or blogs.

Action planning is common sense and at a surface level is very straightforward. The steps can be laid out in a systematic way in order to move from a desired goal to a concrete reality:

What action do I need to take to achieve my desired end point vision?

When shall I start and what is the planned completion date?

Who do I need to support or challenge me?

What resources (time, energy, money, expertise) do I need to access?

How committed am I to taking the required action?

The action plan charts your required behaviour. It could be seen as an act of heroism in that you are taking the risk of seeking to turn your dreams into a reality. This is particularly brave when you are embarking upon a life-changing 'being' goal rather than a simple 'doing' goal. In any case, your plan should meet several criteria. As a result of your planning, you need to be:

Clear — I know exactly what I have to do

Committed — my level of commitment is high (nine or ten)

Organised — the action is summarised as a time-line in my diary

Accountable — to yourself and/or others for the completion of the project

You may find it helpful to elaborate your action plan in your learning journal or to verbalise it to someone you trust. Speaking it out loud provides you with the opportu-

To Do

Personal investment opportunity

Jason Vale, also known as 'the juice master', emphasises commitment at the level of the will. It is not about strength or knowledge, it is about the will. Apathy, doubt, fear and other disempowering emotions may be your close companions or fleeting visitors that impact your level of commitment to taking action. Identify and name these impostors and inner critics and then consign them to the waste-paper bin! Cross them out in your journal and ignore them.

Next, I would like to invite you to identify your 'mastermind group'. These are the people who support and challenge you, who increase your capacity to take action:

Who are they?

How do they provide support and/or challenge?

When did you last seek their help?

It may be that you would like to increase the size and range of your 'mastermind group'. You could approach people you interact with and/or you could build a virtual group. Put yourself in the shoes of Nelson Mandela or Mother Teresa or Ruby Wax — what questions would they pose to deepen and broaden your thinking? Just for fun try out a virtual coach: choose somebody you find interesting and ask yourself questions from what you imagine to be their perspective.

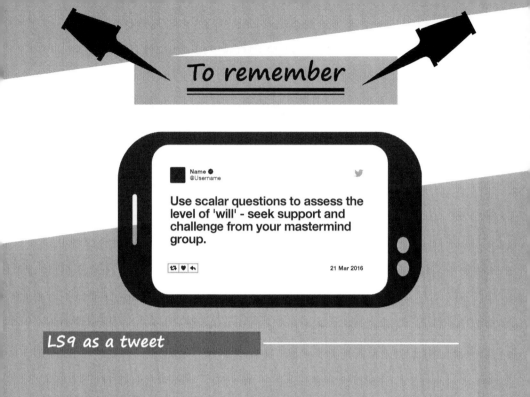

Name ●
@Username

Use scalar questions to assess the level of 'will' - seek support and challenge from your mastermind group.

21 Mar 2016

LS9 as a tweet

nity to 'hear' what you are planning and to decide whether you want to effect any modifications. The other person will, by design or default, provide a mirror for you to reflect on the viability of your plan.

LEARNING STEP 10

What have you learned in studying Module 1?

LS10 is designed to help you:

* pause, draw breath and review your learning
* review the nine golden threads of Module 1
* answer the review questions
* revisit the objectives of the LaCL Programme

Module 1 LS10

LIVING
A
COACHING
LIFESTYLE

Module 1

LS10 What have you learned in studying Module 1?

LS9 Can you translate your goals into concrete action?

LS8 What best options exist for your life's next phase?

LS7 What is your current reality?

LS6 Are you setting the agenda for your own life?

LS5 Can you use a simple model to live a coaching lifestyle?

LS4 How can you release more of your true potential?

LS2 What are your current goals?

LS3 What do you believe about your own potential?

LS1 Where are you now?

Module 1: Designing the plans — employing the GROW model

What have you learned in studying Module 1?

Learning is a treasure that will follow its owner everywhere. (Chinese Proverb)

The only way that we can live, is if we grow. The only way that we can grow is if we change. The only way that we can change is if we learn. The only way we can learn is if we are exposed. And the only way that we can become exposed is if we throw ourselves out into the open. Do it. Throw yourself. (C. JoyBell C. — American thinker, writer and mentor)

Congratulations! You are on the tenth learning step, one third of the way through the programme. Pause here for a moment, draw breath, have a look around and review your learning. You have addressed nine questions so far:

LS1: Where are you now?

LS2: What are your current goals?

LS3: What do you believe about your own potential?

LS4: How can you release more of your true potential?

LS5: Can you use a simple model to live a coaching lifestyle?

LS6: Are you setting the agenda for your own life?

LS7: What is your current reality?

LS8: What best options exist for your life's next phase?

LS9: Can you translate your goals into concrete action?

This module has been designed to introduce you to the notion of **living a coaching lifestyle**. When my middle daughter was a medical student she had access to a cadaver, a body that had been donated to medical science. The decision for her and her colleagues was to decide where to make the first incision in order to maximise the learning experience. I have had the same challenge in preparing this material. There is much to gain from coaching but

73

where to start? I have endeavoured to weave nine basic concepts into the first nine learning steps — the golden threads of this first module:

» reflection as a growth activity

» capturing your reflective thinking in a learning journal

» your 'stage of life'

» 'doing' and 'being'

» the 'wheel of life'

» establishing your personal and professional goals

» the GROW model

» the reticular activating system (RAS)

» your 'mastermind group'

These concepts have popped up at various points in the text and personal investment opportunities. I would like to invite you to record your current understanding of each of these golden threads in your journal and I have designed the following questions to focus your thinking.

The opening quotation in this Learning Step, the Chinese

Review questions	
1	How much time and energy have you invested in reflecting on the nine learning steps? What have you noticed about your ability to reflect?
2	What does your journal tell you about your learning so far?
3	How would you define your current 'Stage of Life'?
4	How would you differentiate between 'doing' and 'being'?
5	Look back at the 'Wheel of Life' exercise (LS2) — what progress have you made on the goals you identified?
6	What are your current top personal and professional goals?
7	What have you learned about using the GROW model?
8	What is your understanding of the reticular activating system (RAS)?
9	Who is in your 'mastermind group'?

74

Table 7 Module 1 review questions

proverb, emphasises that learning is an investment that will continue to produce rich rewards. I am not sure why you chose to embark on this programme and what you hoped to gain from it. My fervent hope is that you will find it a very high-return investment that continues to support your learning.

As I outlined in the Introduction, my reasons for writing the **living a coaching lifestyle** programme are summarised in the following four objectives.

» To introduce you to the core skills of coaching.

» To provide you with opportunities to develop these coaching skills, both for your own good and for the good of others.

» To encourage you to enjoy change at home and at work.

» To consider living a coaching lifestyle.

Reflect on the review questions set out opposite in Table 7 and use your responses as the launch pad for Module 2.

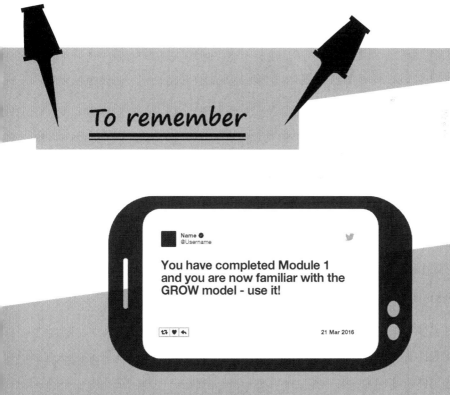

To remember

Name ✔
@Username

You have completed Module 1 and you are now familiar with the GROW model - use it!

21 Mar 2016

LS10 as a tweet

Notes

What is a coaching lifestyle?

LS11 is designed to help you:

* define your version of a coaching lifestyle
* make the most of every opportunity
* understand 'unconscious competence'
* realise the power of the role model

Module 2 LS11

LIVING
A
COACHING
LIFESTYLE

Module 2

Module 2: Laying the foundations — developing the core skills

LS20 What have you learned in studying Module 2?

LS19 How good are you at managing yourself?

LS18 What should you say when you talk to yourself?

LS17 What core values support your life's vision?

LS16 Are you committed to developing a coaching lifestyle?

LS15 Who provides you with support and challenge?

LS14 Can you transform plans into action?

LS12 How good is your listening?

LS13 What is the quality of the questions you are posing?

LS11 What is a coaching lifestyle?

What is a coaching lifestyle?

Opportunity dances with those who are already on the dance floor. (H Jackson Brown Jr. — American author and inspirational speaker)

My personal answer to the above question can be summarised in four bullet points. A coaching lifestyle involves:

» conducting your life in a conscious, mindful state

» nurturing curiosity and investigative awareness

» being open-minded and prepared to seize opportunities when they present themselves

» using coaching skills and techniques in consciously and unconsciously competent ways.

Life is an adventure to be lived. The Latin phrase *Carpe diem* literally means 'seize the day'. This imperative is at the heart of a coaching lifestyle — focus on this day and get the most you possibly can out of it.

This programme started out as a core primer in the development of the skills required to coach other people and has transformed itself into a way of living your own unique existence. I believe I will pass this way once only and I want to make the most of it. I don't want to depart this life regretting missed opportunities as I didn't have the will to be '**living a coaching lifestyle**'. The world is teeming with opportunities, we just have to learn to recognise them and take the appropriate action.

H Jackson Brown Jr. suggests that we have to be in the right state to make the most of the opportunities that present themselves. Firstly we need to be able to recognise the potential dance partner of opportunity and then we need the courage to ask for the dance. The reticular activating system needs to be fully open to spot potential partners and see the opportunities inherent in the dance.

The core skills at the heart of a coaching lifestyle are:

» listening for understanding

» questioning for depth and breadth

» promoting conscious action

» engaging with the twin pillars of support and challenge.

A good listener will always be popular and successful because we all enjoy talking about our favourite subject — ourselves. Listening is a skill that when applied generatively will have a significant impact in the workplace. It would seem equally as important to maximise this core skill in our interactions with family and friends.

We show the quality of care we have for people by the way we listen to them. The research on self-talk identifies that the person I listen to most of all is myself. Do I deserve my own loving attention?

Questioning others is a sensitive and skilful business. The knack is to locate the right question at just the right moment. A good question posed at the opportune time will deepen and broaden the thinking of the person you are speaking to. In the same way, asking myself the 'right question' at the right moment will have a galvanising effect upon the quality of my own thinking.

Raising these questions to a conscious level provides the opportunity to stop and take stock and to plan a course of action. On occasions, it may be helpful to engage the help of someone you trust to pose the challenging questions you have avoided asking yourself. When to involve another person is a judgement call.

All meaningful change requires conscious action. If I continue to do what I have habitually done, I will continue to get what I have always got! (See LS9) A coaching lifestyle

Unconscious incompetence 'The blissful state of unawarenesss'	Conscious incompetence 'An uncomfortable state of awareness'
Conscious competence 'Working hard at a new behaviour'	Unconscious competence 'Success without thinking about it'

Figure 3 Dubin's Dichotomies

Level	Listening quality	Description
1	Unconscious incompetence	I am not aware that I cannot drive/ Learning to drive has not occurred to me.
2	Conscious incompetence	I know I cannot do it yet, and I want to learn it/ Or, I am learning it but I have not yet got the hang of it.
3	Conscious competence	I know what to do know: let's see...clutch down...into first gear...a little bit of accelerator... clutch up.
4	Unconscious competence	How did I get here? I am not consciously thinking about driving.

Table 8 Dichotomies in learning to drive

involves taking planned action in a systematic and competent way. We are seeking to develop habits that serve us rather than sabotage us. Dubin's dichotomies is a helpful learning model that illustrates this concept (Figure 3). The four stages of competence — learning to drive as an example could be illustrated as this representation (Table 8).

We can coach ourselves and others from 'unconscious incompetence' through to 'unconscious competence'. We may need a mixture of support and challenge to facilitate this learning journey. Indeed, the twin pillars of support and challenge are central to a coaching lifestyle. There will be times when you need insightful support and other times when you require raw challenge. The clever bit is to be able to recognise the times and to know whose help to seek. Your 'mastermind group' should contain people who will support you and people who will challenge you and some invaluable characters who can do both.

I choose where to invest my attention and energy. A coaching lifestyle involves consciously adopting an open-minded, questioning approach to the events of each precious day. The biggest impact I have on the people I live and work with is the nature of my role model. My actions are far more eloquent than my words. Indeed, it could be argued that investing in myself is an altruistic endeavour that will have positive consequences for the people around me. The benefits of a coaching lifestyle will spill over into the lives of the people I live and work with and will add quality to my own existence.

To Do

Personal investment opportunity

* What is your definition of a coaching lifestyle?

* Are you on the dance floor and seeking to identify the opportunities that present themselves as potential partners?

* Identify three unhelpful habits you would like to change — coach yourself through the stages of Dubin's dichotomies.

To remember

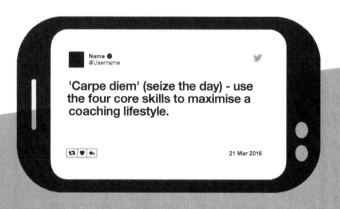

Name
@Username

'Carpe diem' (seize the day) - use the four core skills to maximise a coaching lifestyle.

21 Mar 2016

LS11 as a tweet

LEARNING STEP 12

How good is your listening?

LS12 is designed to help you:

* listen for understanding
* understand the enormous power of listening
* differentiate the four levels
* see that listening is a way of serving people

Module 2 LS12

LIVING
A
COACHING
LIFESTYLE

Module 2

Module 2: Laying the foundations — developing the core skills

LS20 What have you learned in studying Module 2?

LS19 How good are you at managing yourself?

LS18 What should you say when you talk to yourself?

LS17 What core values support your life's vision?

LS16 Are you committed to developing a coaching lifestyle?

LS15 Who provides you with support and challenge?

LS14 Can you transform plans into action?

LS12 How good is your listening?

LS13 What is the quality of the questions you are posing?

LS11 What is a coaching lifestyle?

How good is your listening?

We show the quality of our care for people by the way we listen to them. (Barbara Ward — health educator and Cruse counsellor)

The next four learning steps elaborate the core skills of a coaching lifestyle:

» Listening for understanding

» Questioning for depth

» Promoting action

» Maximising support and challenge.

Listening is a vital life skill, it is at the heart of almost everything we do. We spend a large part of our waking hours engaged in the business of listening, either to others or to ourselves. It is the first key element of a coaching lifestyle because it creates an environment for change. At the very least, listening can be seen as the highest form of courtesy as you are conferring your attention and interest on the speaker. Indeed, for some parts of the day, the speaker may be yourself and you deserve that same level of attention you would accord to someone else.

Level	Listening quality	Description
1	Surface listening	Listening from habit, meaningless chatter and social 'buzz' (closed mind)
2	Factual listening	Paying attention and noticing differences that could be useful or important later (open mind)
3	Empathic listening	Connecting at an emotional level and seeing the world through the eyes of the speaker (open heart)
4	Generative listening	Ability to connect with an emerging future and the shifting identity of the speaker (open will)

Table 9 Listening quality

The quality of our listening ebbs and flows for a variety of reasons, such as our level of tiredness, the nature of the topic or the skill of the speaker. The judgement call is to decide when to unleash our highest level listening in order to make sense of the world, plan the future or build positive social relationships. The quality of our listening changes with the amount of focused effort we direct towards what we are listening to. It is a tiring activity and so learning where to invest our 'best listening' will pay dividends.

The notion of employing different 'levels of listening' provides a useful working model (Table 9, Table 10).

The opening quotation from Barbara Ward captures an essential truth in the coaching process — listening creates

Level 1	Level 2
Level 1 listening is superficial and does not require any significant investment of energy. It is designed to oil the wheels of social intercourse. On occasion, the other person may not need your committed attention, you are simply the excuse for them to let off steam or think aloud.	Level 2 listening involves paying attention and processing the information being shared. The intention is to stay focused on the speaker and to understand what is being communicated. The listener is mentally registering and recording facts so that they can be used later if necessary.

Table 10 Levels of listening

the environment for systematic reflection and progressive thinking to flourish. Barbara Ward was both an esteemed colleague and an empathic Cruse Bereavement Counsellor and she personified the power of high quality listening. She believed that it is impossible to care for others if you do not care for yourself first.

Good listeners will always be popular because we all like to be listened to. The starting point for effective listening is for the listener to have the best interests of the speaker at the centre of what is happening. As a listening coach we are seeking to serve the speaker, whether that is a family member, close friend, work colleague or self!

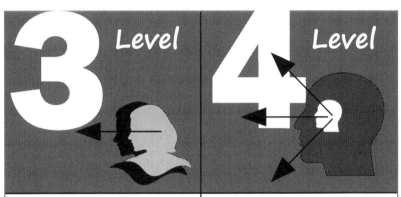

Level 3 listening moves into a deeper level and requires emotional connection.	Level 4 listening goes beyond what is usually possible and is almost telepathic.
A North American Indian saying holds that "You cannot understand another person until you have walked a journey in their moccasins".	Generative listening involves a finely tuned ability to understand the other person and to be fully focussed on them rather than self. The mind of the listener is quiet, calm and in a state of relaxed concentration.
Empathic listening enables the listener to see the world through the speaker's eyes and to understand their 'current reality'.	This level of listening facilitates new insights in the speaker.

To Do

Personal investment opportunity

Over the next week:

* Log examples of listening to other people at all four levels. The first two levels will be relatively straight-forward, the second two will probably require a bit more effort. Reflect on how you move up and down the levels.

* Log examples of listening to yourself at all four levels. This activity may feel a little unnatural but persevere anyway and record what happens.

To remember

Name ✔
@Username

Listening to yourself and others is a vital skill that creates an environment for systematic reflection.

21 Mar 2016

LS12 as a tweet

What is the quality of the questions you are posing?

LS13 is designed to help you:

* adopt a questioning approach to life

* pose the right question at the right time

* use questions to broaden and deepen your thinking

* use questions to support the planning process

Module 2 LS13

LIVING
A
COACHING
LIFESTYLE

Module 2

LS20 What have
you learned in
studying
Module 2?

LS19 How good are
you at managing
yourself?

LS18 What should
you say when you
talk to yourself?

LS17 What core values
support your life's vision?

LS16 Are you committed
to developing a coaching
lifestyle?

LS15 Who pro-
vides you with
support and
challenge?

LS14 Can you
transform plans
into action?

LS12 How
good is your
listening?

LS13 What is the quality of
the questions you are posing?

LS11 What is a
coaching lifestyle?

What is the quality of the questions you are posing?

You can tell whether a man is clever by his answers. You can tell whether a man is wise by his questions. (Naguib Mahfouz — Egyptian writer and Nobel Prize for Literature winner)

A coaching lifestyle is characterised by a questioning approach to all we think and do. As rehearsed in LS12, we listen in order to understand and make sense of what is going on. Asking the right question at the right moment often provides the key to unlocking a complex situation. Indeed, framing a well-chosen question will help you to:

» clarify your goal

» explore your current thinking and feeling

» generate a breadth and depth of options

» build commitment to taking action

» give focus to the coaching dialogue.

Young children ask question after question and this is how they learn about themselves and the world around them. As adults we can choose to perpetuate this enquiring approach and to consciously develop our questioning technique. There are many taxonomies of questioning types in the literature and I have endeavoured to summarise the genres I employ as a coach in Table 11 below.

Question genre	Example of this type of question
Ideal outcome	What would it be like if it was perfect?
Situational	What, why, when, how, where and who?
Sensory	How does that sound? (look or feel)
Implication	What would happen if...?
"Columbo"	(television detective) How does that work?
No constraints	If you knew you couldn't fail, what would you do?
Motivation	How committed are you on a scale of 1 to 10?

Table 11 Question genres

The coaching dialogue could be viewed as 'a game of two halves'. In the first half the questions are designed to encourage a breadth and depth of divergent thinking, while in the second half the best option is transformed into a workable action plan (convergent thinking). In other words, we go as wide as possible in order to generate a range of options and then narrow to develop a plan of action for the best option. Table 12 simplifies the process and thus does not do justice to the richness and complexity of the coaching dialogue, but it is a conceptual starting point.

Stage in the process	Questioning designed to...
Goal	Define a clear goal (start)
Exploration	Broaden and deepen thinking and feeling (widen)
Options	Capture the best options (pause)
Evaluation	Evaluate each option and select (narrow)
Action	Commit to action (act)

Table 12 Questioning process stages

High quality questioning is a performing art and any attempt to systematise a pre-planned strategy could be viewed as reductionist. Having said that, it is helpful to have some insights to help you analyse what is required next in the coaching process. 'Blind coaching' emphasises the nature of the questioning without any feedback from the respondent and lays bare the backbone of the coaching process. A very simple thread of questioning might run like this:

» What is your goal for this project?

» What is the current reality?

» What are your best three options?

» What is your best option?

» How committed are you to taking the action?

We could employ a variety of questioning genres at various stages in the process. For example:

» **G stage:** You have said your goal is.... What would that be like if it was perfect? (ideal outcome question)

» **R stage**: The current state of play is.... How does that look or feel to you? (sensory question)

» **O stage:** You have said.... How does that work? ("Columbo" Question)

» **W stage:** On a scale of 1 - 10 how committed are you to taking the action? (scalar question).

To conclude, coaching questions can be pre-planned and designed to navigate your way around the GROW model or they can be spontaneous and opportunistic, reflecting the quality of your listening. To quote Naguib Mah-

To Do

Personal investment opportunity

Over the next week:

Log examples of the questions you ask other people. Analyse these questions in terms of genre and impact.

Log examples of the questions you ask yourself, again in terms of genre and impact.

Consciously seek to broaden and deepen your questioning strategies. Rehearse the different genres with yourself and others.

Empty your mind and resist the temptation to frame a question while the other person is speaking. Maintain an attitude of relaxed concentration and listen deeply to what they are saying and then frame a question that

* follows their interest

* uses their words

* is succinct.

fouz, the Egyptian author, the best questions demonstrate the wisdom of the questioner. The questions follow the respondent's interest and are framed using their own words. These questions are also usually succinct and neutral. Self-coaching is a major challenge in terms of posing questions that are both objective and neutral. I have to confess to occasionally falling into the trap of asking myself the questions that will produce the outcome I desire. This is called self-deception and is not fully **living a coaching lifestyle**.

To remember

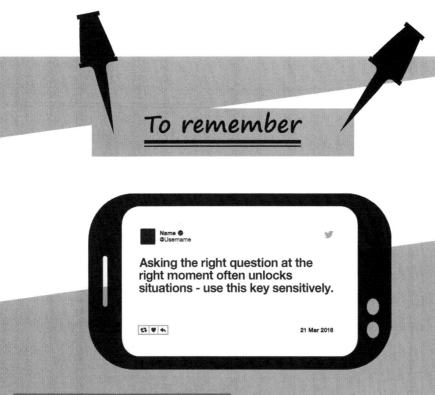

Name ●
@Username

Asking the right question at the right moment often unlocks situations - use this key sensitively.

21 Mar 2016

LS13 as a tweet

Can you transform plans into action?

LS14 is designed to help you:

* turn plans into concrete action

* generate commitment to the planned action

* test the utility of the plan

* evaluate commitment at the level of the will

Module 2 LS14

LIVING
A
COACHING
LIFESTYLE

Module 2

Module 2: Laying the foundations – developing the core skills

LS20 What have you learned in studying Module 2?

LS19 How good are you at managing yourself?

LS18 What should you say when you talk to yourself?

LS17 What core values support your life's vision?

LS16 Are you committed to developing a coaching lifestyle?

LS15 Who provides you with support and challenge?

LS14 Can you transform plans into action?

LS12 How good is your listening?

LS13 What is the quality of the questions you are posing?

LS11 What is a coaching lifestyle?

Can you transform plans into action?

At the end of the day, you are solely responsible for your success and your failure. And the sooner you realise that, you accept that, and integrate that into your work ethic, you will start being successful. (Erin Cummings — American actress)

Listening and questioning are the golden skills at the heart of a coaching lifestyle. A right application of these skills will generate a range of elegant action plans that provide a warm glow of anticipation. However, these plans are worthless unless they are turned into concrete action. A coaching lifestyle should be evaluated in terms of the impact of the action it generates. **Promoting action** is the third core skill.

In LS13 we explored the five stages in the coaching process (Table 13).

Stage in the process	Questioning designed to...
Goal	Define a clear goal (start)
Exploration	Broaden and deepen thinking and feeling (widen)
Options	Capture the best options (pause)
Evaluation	Evaluate each option and select (narrow)
Action	Commit to action (act)

Table 13 Questioning process stages

The action plan emerges from the previous four stages, although progress through the stages is rarely a nice clean, linear process. There is often movement up and down the model as clarity is sought. Appropriate investment in exploring current reality and generating options will expedite the evaluation and action planning stages. Ultimately a clear plan of action emerges and procrastination issues and other blockages have been addressed. In short, there is now a high level of commitment to take the required action.

At this point it is worthwhile applying four simple tests

97

Test	Evidence
1. Clarity	I know exactly what I need to do
2. Commitment	On a scale of 1-10, I am at 8, 9 or preferably 10!
3. Diary	The action is broken down into a clear time-line
4. Deadline	I am committed to completing the action by...

Table 14 Evaluation and evidence in actioning

to evaluate the utility of the action that has been planned (Table 14).

Erin Cummings, an American actress, in the above quotation emphasises the importance of us taking responsibility for both our successes and failures. The maxim 'If it is to be, it is down to me' is helpful in this context. Of course we can benefit from the support and challenge of other people, but the primary responsibility for taking the required action resides firmly with me. This is an empowering starting point and is potentially transformational in terms of turning our plans into meaningful action.

Many people dream both by day and by night and in order to turn these dreams into reality something has to be changed. I repeat yet again, if you always do what you have always done, you will always get what you have always got. It is the triumph of hope over reality if you keep doing the same thing and hope for a different outcome. Dreams are just that, unless you are prepared to translate them into concrete action. A coaching lifestyle will encourage us to be more reflective and to become more aware of our dreams and aspirations. The coaching process provides a framework for making things happen. Trust the process.

A personal commitment to taking the planned action is the launch pad to success. This may require changed behaviours and sustained effort if the dream is to become a reality. There are a variety of strategies for building commitment to action.

Remind myself that I have chosen this action as a result of investing in the coaching process — it is

To Do

Personal investment opportunity

Undertake an honest self appraisal and seek answers to the following questions:

* How good am I at translating plans into concrete action?

* What procrastination strategies do I employ that reduce my readiness to take action?

* Where can I apply the maxim "If it is to be, it is down to me"?

* Can I begin to see the impact of a coaching lifestyle on my behaviour?

To remember

Name
@Username

A coaching lifestyle can be evaluated by the action it generates - check clarity, commitment, diary and deadline.

21 Mar 2016

LS14 as a tweet

'my' action, it is not being imposed.

I have verbalised the action to a trusted other and heard myself elaborate the plan.

I have gone public with my commitment at the level of the will — a score of 8, 9 or preferably 10.

I have written it down in my reflective learning log and laid out the time-line in my diary.

I am responsible for the outcome of the action and I am accountable to myself!

As Erin Cummings says, I am solely responsible!

Who provides you with support and challenge?

LS15 is designed to help you:

* understand the power of support and challenge

* broaden your 'master-mind group'

* find the right balance in any situation

* seek the support and challenge you need

Module 2 LS15

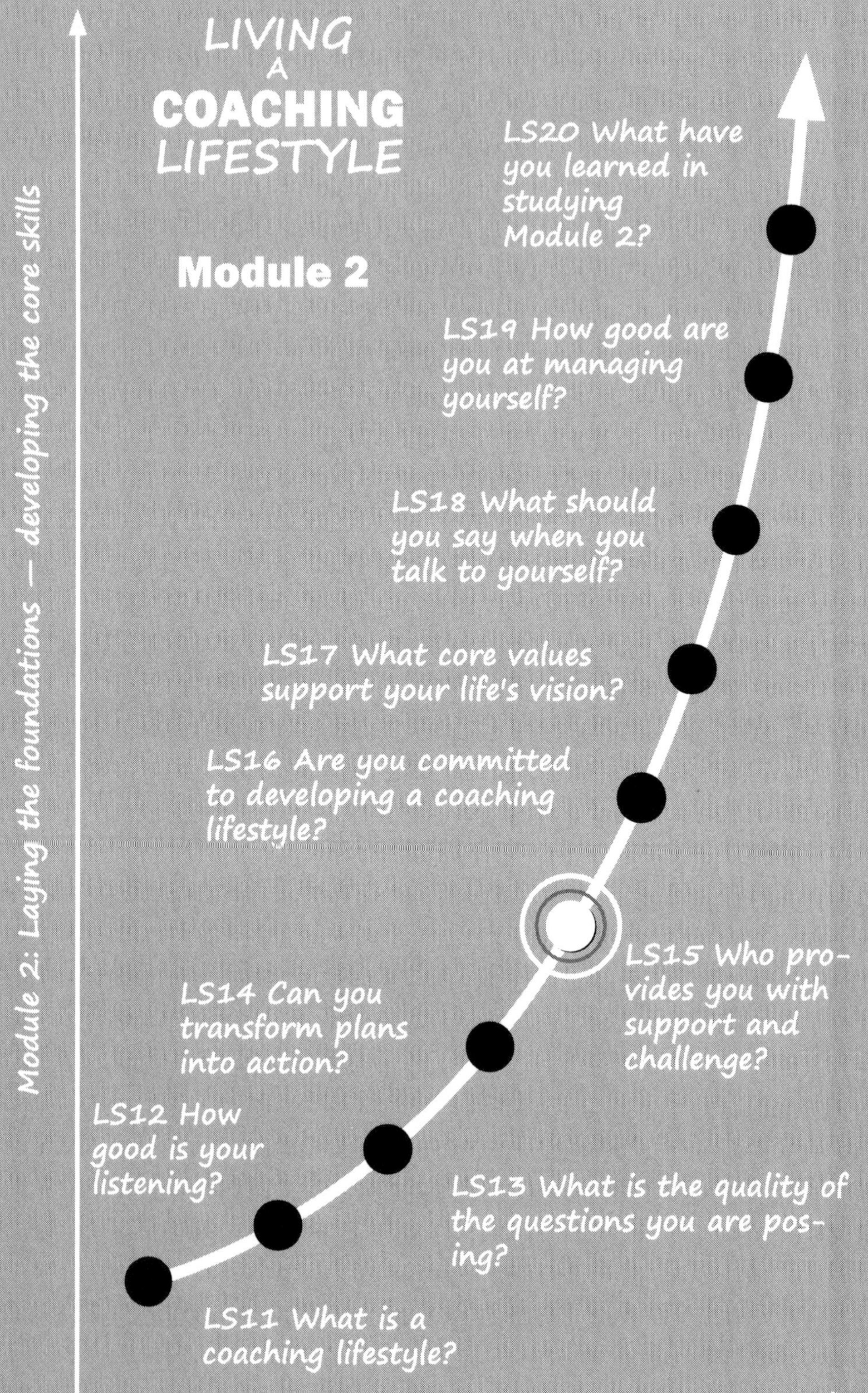

LIVING
A
COACHING
LIFESTYLE

Module 2

LS20 What have
you learned in
studying
Module 2?

LS19 How good are
you at managing
yourself?

LS18 What should
you say when you
talk to yourself?

LS17 What core values
support your life's vision?

LS16 Are you committed
to developing a coaching
lifestyle?

LS15 Who pro-
vides you with
support and
challenge?

LS14 Can you
transform plans
into action?

LS12 How
good is your
listening?

LS13 What is the quality of
the questions you are posing?

LS11 What is a
coaching lifestyle?

Who provides you with support and challenge?

> You are the average of the five people you spend the most time with. (Jim Rohn — American entrepreneur, author and motivational speaker)

A coaching lifestyle is enhanced by having a network of people who provide you with the support and challenge that will help you develop. Those nearest and dearest to you may provide either support or challenge, or indeed both. Relying on one or two people to discharge this function though, may be both unrealistic and unfair to your loved ones. In my view, it is desirable to spread the load over a wider network and to enlist the help of a range of people you respect and trust. Broaden your 'mastermind group' (see LS9), so that you can seek support or challenge from specialists or enlist the help of a mixture of people with different perspectives.

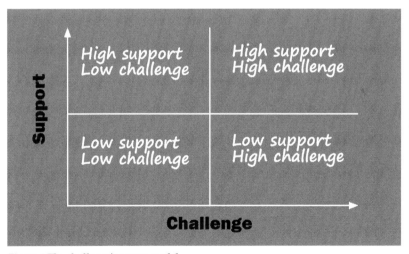

Figure 4 The challenge/support model

Effective support and challenge structures are the fourth element of a coaching lifestyle. Running up 'change hill' is enhanced by having a committed back-up team of spectators who offer encouragement, inspiration and the odd drink of water. What is the current reality of the balance of support and challenge in your life? Look at the model depicted in Figure 4 above.

103

The top right quadrant provides an ideal balance of high support and high challenge. The judgement call is to sense when you need to ask for support and when you need to seek challenge. Your needs will shift and change in relation to the nature of the task you are undertaking.

The bottom right quadrant is not a comfortable place. The level of challenge is high and you may feel as if you are in a lonely place without the support structures you need. In the style of a reckless trapeze artist, you are working without a net.

The top left quadrant is 'easy street'. You have huge support but insufficient challenge. This can be a very boring place to be as you are denied the enjoyment and stimulation of testing yourself and you are not investing in your own growth.

The bottom left quadrant is the worst of all worlds. You have the double disappointment of feeling both unsupported and lacking personal or professional challenge. This is a place of stasis. Why get out of bed?

I believe it is our responsibility to seek the support and challenge we need. We can celebrate both significant successes and noble failures when we have been brave enough to **'live a coaching lifestyle'**. Thoughtful dialogue partners can support this process by providing us with unconditional positive regard, while at the same time maintaining an appropriate level of challenge. Ideally their contributions will be both respectful and developmental. These relationships pre-suppose that high levels of trust and openness already exist. Your interactions with members of your mastermind group should be characterised by a balance of stimulation, affirmation and celebration.

One significant element of developing a coaching lifestyle is my willingness to make myself accountable for the outcomes of my actions. The accountability for my actions is:

» Voluntary – I choose to be accountable to myself and members of my mastermind group.

» Positive – I make a conscious choice to focus on the positive.

» Consistent – a habit change requires consistent commitment over a minimum of six weeks.

» Honest – my interactions are predicated on honesty on all sides.

» Specific – it is succinct and to the point.

» Energising – it is about support rather than threat.

To Do

Personal investment opportunity

Jim Rohn was an American entrepreneur, author and motivational speaker. He modelled commitment to his own development and his example had a significant impact upon many people. Do you agree with the idea at the heart of his quotation?

Look again at your mastermind group:

* Where does your support come from?
* Where does your challenge come from?
* Is the balance right?
* Would you like to widen the membership of this group?
* Who might you approach?

Identify a goal you are about to embark upon:

* Who will you enlist to provide support?
* Who will you enlist to provide challenge?
* Who might provide both?
* Examine your own life in terms of resilience and the opportunity to thrive:
* What do I do that increases my personal resilience?
* What do I do that decreases my personal resilience?
* What action grows out of these analyses? Record your answers in your learning journal.

To remember

Name ✓
@Username

You need people who provide you with support and challenge - seek stimulation, affirmation and celebration.

21 Mar 2016

LS15 as a tweet

LEARNING STEP 16

Are you committed to developing a coaching lifestyle?

LS16 is designed to help you:

* evaluate your commitment to LaCL

* reflect on the skill/will matrix

* accelerate into the top right quadrant

* review the core skills of the programme

Module 2 LS16

LIVING
A
COACHING
LIFESTYLE

Module 2

Module 2: Laying the foundations — developing the core skills

LS20 What have you learned in studying Module 2?

LS19 How good are you at managing yourself?

LS18 What should you say when you talk to yourself?

LS17 What core values support your life's vision?

LS16 Are you committed to developing a coaching lifestyle?

LS15 Who provides you with support and challenge?

LS14 Can you transform plans into action?

LS12 How good is your listening?

LS13 What is the quality of the questions you are posing?

LS11 What is a coaching lifestyle?

Are you committed to developing a coaching lifestyle?

Coaching is not merely a technique to be wheeled out and rigidly applied in certain prescribed circumstances. It is a way of managing, a way of treating people, a way of thinking, a way of being. (John Whitmore — author, performance coach and former racing driver)

You are now half way through the programme. Module 2 opened with a discussion of *What is a coaching lifestyle?* (LS11). The following four learning steps elaborated the core skills at the heart of a coaching lifestyle:

» listening for understanding (LS12)

» questioning for depth and breadth (LS13)

» promoting conscious action (LS14)

» engaging with the twin pillars of support and challenge (LS15).

The following four learning steps will focus on how to create the conditions to enable a coaching lifestyle to flourish:

» an analysis of your level of skill and your level of will (LS16)

» values (LS17)

» self-talk (LS18)

» self-management (LS19).

One of my favourite four-quadrant models is the skill/will matrix. It captures an essential truth about success, namely it involves a winning combination of both skill and will. You have studied the four core skills of coaching in the last four learning steps and you now have the ability to apply these skills to your life and work. The key is your level of desire to actually apply theses golden skills. How committed are you at the level of the will to making this knowledge work for you?

The skill/will matrix model is depicted in Figure 5.

The aim of this programme is to accelerate you into the top right quadrant, in other words you are living a coach-

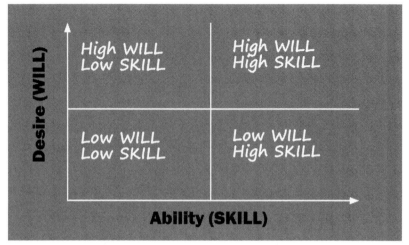

Figure 5 The skill/will matrix

ing lifestyle that is characterised by a high level of will and a high level of skill. In LS9 I identified the fourth part of the GROW model as the will stage. My reason for calling it the will stage is because your commitment at the level of your will is the key determinant of success!

Scalar questions, using numbers or other measures, are helpful in terms of ascertaining your true level of commitment. Ask yourself the following scalar question in relation to your desire to live a coaching lifestyle: "On a scale of one to ten, with one being low and ten being high, how committed am I to taking the necessary action to achieve this goal?"

The GROW model (LS 5 to 9) and the four core skills of coaching (LS 12 to 15) elaborated in the previous learning steps should have provided you with the basis of developing high skill.

Arguably the top left quadrant is also a positive place to be. You are highly committed, but lacking the honed skills to promote a coaching lifestyle. The answer is simple, you need more practice. Your daily life at home and at work is teeming with a myriad of opportunities to practise your coaching skills. Remember the mantra 'the more I practise the luckier I get'. Try things out and reflect on the outcomes. Ask yourself developmental coaching questions and commit yourself to what you will do next time. 'Next time I will...'

The bottom right quadrant suggests that you have an attitude problem. You possess all the relevant skills but choose not to exercise them. This deficit of will suggests a lack of real commitment to action. 'I would like the desired outcome but I am too unsure or too lazy to take the action necessary.' Doing the same thing and expecting a different outcome is the triumph of hope over reality. A different outcome requires a change of behaviour. This is where your commitment at the level of the will really kicks in!

If you are in the bottom left quadrant, low will and low skill, you are probably investing in the wrong programme and wasting your time. You are neither willing nor able and living a coaching lifestyle is a remote possibility. If you have employed people who inhabit this quadrant, encourage them to leave as soon as possible and in the

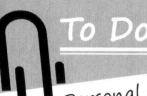

To Do

Personal investment opportunity

Reflect on the skill/will matrix and where you are in the development of a coaching lifestyle

Give yourself a score out of ten on the core skills (one is low, ten is high):

* listening for understanding

* questioning for depth and breadth

* promoting conscious action

* engaging with the twin pillars of support and challenge

Give yourself a score out of ten for your level of commitment to developing a coaching lifestyle

meantime tell them exactly what you want them to do. Do not encourage them to use their initiative because they have not got any!

Sir John Whitmore is the author of *Coaching for Performance*[1], the best-selling coaching book in circulation and a pre-eminent leadership thinker. His quotation at the beginning of this learning step indicates that coaching is all encompassing, "it is a way of managing, a way of treating people, a way of thinking, a way of being." In short it is a lifestyle choice.

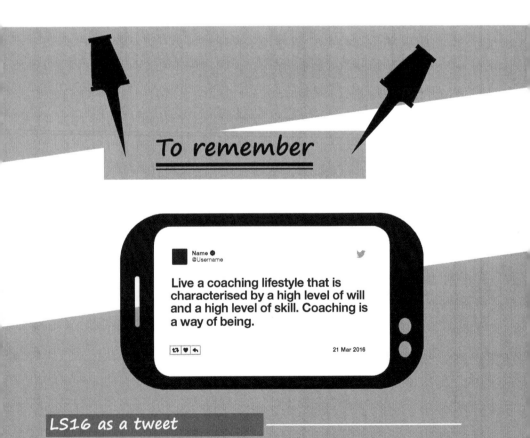

To remember

Name ●
@Username

Live a coaching lifestyle that is characterised by a high level of will and a high level of skill. Coaching is a way of being.

21 Mar 2016

LS16 as a tweet

LEARNING STEP 17

What core values support your life's vision?

LS17 is designed to help you:

* clarify your core values
* understand the power of your value base
* articulate a personal vision and mission
* commit to your conclusions in writing

Module 2 LS17

LIVING
A
COACHING
LIFESTYLE

Module 2

LS20 What have
you learned in
studying
Module 2?

LS19 How good are
you at managing
yourself?

LS18 What should
you say when you
talk to yourself?

LS17 What core values
support your life's vision?

LS16 Are you committed
to developing a coaching
lifestyle?

LS15 Who pro-
vides you with
support and
challenge?

LS14 Can you
transform plans
into action?

LS12 How
good is your
listening?

LS13 What is the quality of
the questions you are posing?

LS11 What is a
coaching lifestyle?

Module 2: Laying the foundations — developing the core skills

What core values support your life's vision?

It's the job of any business owner to be clear about the company's non-negotiable core values. They're the riverbanks that help guide us as we refine and improve on performance and excellence. A lack of riverbanks creates estuaries and cloudy waters that are confusing to navigate. I want a crystal-clear, swiftly flowing stream. (Danny Meyer — American restaurateur and Chief Executive Officer)

The quotation above asserts that it is important for a business to be clear about its non-negotiable core values. I believe that it is even more important for us as individuals to be clear about the values that are informing our lives. I would prefer to navigate a crystal clear, swiftly flowing stream, rather than the cloudy waters of an estuary!

It is rare for people to raise their core values to the conscious level. It may happen to a degree in selection interviews, but then we may not always be completely transparent in those unnatural situations. Nevertheless, it is worth investing time in reflecting upon the values that drive us and inform our life choices. Values underpin everything we do.

Just over two years ago, I finally got around to committing my core values to paper. I started by reflecting on the vision and mission for my life and the behaviours these would engender. It was then a logical next step to identify the values that drive that vision, mission and resulting behaviours. The finished article is now prominently displayed in my study in order to remind myself that these values are at the core of my life and should inform all my behavioural choices.

The following summary of my finished document is included as a possible template, or at least as a starting point for your own deliberations. Focus on the headings and respond in whatever way feels appropriate. Here goes:

My vision: To help people be the best they can be

115

My mission: To support and challenge people to grow, perform and gain satisfaction and enjoyment from what they do

In order to achieve my vision and mission I will:

* *encourage*

* *inspire*

* *coach*

* *educate*

* *I will support this by:*
  » *managing my own self-talk*
  » *being ruthlessly optimistic*
  » *feeding my mind through prayer, reflection, reading and coaching*
  » *being a life-long learner*

* *The core values that drive me are:*
  » *integrity*
  » *wisdom*
  » *serenity*

Martin Seligman in his book entitled *Flourish*[1] offers us open access to the *Values in Action Signature Strengths Test* (VIA). This test and an interpretation of the results can be obtained from his *Authentic Happiness* website, at *www.authentichappiness.org*. This website is free and has been designed as a public service. Almost 2 million people have registered at the website and taken the tests. The goals of the programme are to help people identify their signature strengths and to increase their use of these signature strengths in their daily lives.

Clear core values support a coaching lifestyle as they guide behaviour and expedite decision-making. Articulate them in writing and keep them in full view. Either consciously or unconsciously your core values will inform your friendships and business relationships. Your core values also help you manage yourself (see LS19). In short, core values underpin everything we do. Take the time to clarify exactly what yours are.

To Do

Personal investment opportunity

Mahatma Gandhi said:

Your beliefs become your thoughts.
Your thoughts become your words.
Your words become your actions.
Your actions become your habits.
Your habits become your values.
Your values become your destiny.

My sense is that values come first and inform your thinking, speaking and action. Either way it is important to be clear about what your core values actually are. Try one, two or three of the following activities.

Identify your values — three complementary approaches:

* Use my personal template

* Take the 'Values in Action Signature Strengths Test' (VIA) at www.authentichappiness.org

* Reflect on the following starter questions

Values in action

1. What is most important to you in your life and work?
2. What does this give you/bring you?
3. What else is important in your life and work?
4. What does this give you/bring you?
5. What do you most enjoy doing? (What floats your boat?)
6. What does this give you/bring you?
7. What most annoys you?
8. If this annoys you, if you turn it upside down, what is it that's important to you?

Value	Scoring
1	
2	
3	
4	

Scoring:

Use a scale of 1-10 (1 being not at all in line and 10 being in total alignment)

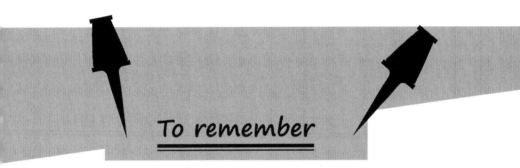

To remember

Name ●
@Username

Values underpin everything we do. Clear core values support a coaching lifestyle as they guide and expedite decision-making.

21 Mar 2016

LS17 as a tweet

What should you say when you talk to yourself?

LS18 is designed to help you:

* review your self-talk
* differentiate negative and positive scripts
* understand the impact of what you say to yourself
* choose the self-talk you want

Module 2 LS18

LIVING
A
COACHING
LIFESTYLE

Module 2

Module 2: Laying the foundations — developing the core skills

LS20 What have you learned in studying Module 2?

LS19 How good are you at managing yourself?

LS18 What should you say when you talk to yourself?

LS17 What core values support your life's vision?

LS16 Are you committed to developing a coaching lifestyle?

LS15 Who provides you with support and challenge?

LS14 Can you transform plans into action?

LS12 How good is your listening?

LS13 What is the quality of the questions you are posing?

LS11 What is a coaching lifestyle?

What should you say when you talk to yourself?

Self-talk gives each of us a way to change what we would like to change. It offers us the chance to stop being the old self and to start to become a different, better self, a self which is no longer the product of conditioned response, but governed instead by personal choice. (Shad Helmstetter — American author and television personality)

The nature of your self-talk has a profound effect upon the quality of your life. Self-talk comes in two basic varieties — negative and positive. Negative self-talk is destructive and engenders disappointment and under-performance. On the other hand, positive self-talk predisposes us to success and generates optimism and resourcefulness. The choice is yours!

Listen to your self-talk scripts in a conscious and deliberate way. Record what you hear in your journal and reflect upon what you have written. Which frequently-run scripts are hampering you and which ones are serving you? These scripts are constructed by your habitual thinking and the prevailing image you hold of yourself. Apparently we each have approximately 50,000 thoughts every day. It would be impossible to capture every thought, but usually there are some strong recurring themes that feature regularly within our inner dialogue.

Self-talk is your mental evaluation of what you have done, what you are doing and what you are about to do. Each conversation you have with yourself and with other people has a potential impact upon your self-image. Some people are more influential than others, but you decide either consciously or unconsciously who is going to influence your thinking. The nature of your self-image predisposes you to particular behaviours. The great news is that you can deliberately choose to increase the percentage of positive, up-building self-talk and at the same time to decrease the amount of negative, destructive self-talk.

Let us revisit Dubin's dichotomies in order to shed light on our habitual self-talk (Figure 6).

Unconscious incompetence	Conscious incompetence
Conscious competence	Unconscious competence

Figure 6 Dubin's Dichotomies

The four stages of competence — the impact of self-talk is shown in Table 15.

Level	Listening quality	Description
1	Unconscious incompetence	I am not aware of my negative self-talk. Changing my self-talk has not occurred to me.
2	Conscious incompetence	I do not manage what I want to say to myself. I am aware of the negative impact of my self-talk.
3	Conscious competence	I know what to say to myself. I focus on up-building self-talk.
4	Unconscious competence	My negative self-talk has decreased. My positive self-talk has increased.

Table 15 Four stages of competence and self-talk

I became aware of the power of self-talk over 25 years ago and I believe it has a major impact upon us at a variety of levels. The nature of the self-talk in your family, or the organisation that employs you, will be a significant influence on the culture that exists there. The prevailing self-talk within your team will also have a massive influence on how it feels to work with those people. Most significantly, the person you talk to most (yourself) will be profoundly impacted by the quality of your self-talk. I say again, the choice is yours!

Shad Helmstetter[1] suggests that there are five separate levels of self-talk (Table 16).

Level	Listening quality	Description
1	The level of negative acceptance "I CAN'T..."	The subconscious mind is listening and acts on negative instructions.
2	The level of recognition and need to change "I SHOULD..."	This level is beguiling: it looks as if it should work, but actually works against us. It creates guilt and disappointment.
3	The level of decision to change "I NEVER...I NO LONGER..."	Remember your subconscious will believe anything if you tell it long enough and strongly enough.
4	The level of better you "I AM..."	This is the most effective self-talk we can ever use.
5	The level of universal affirmation "IT IS..."	This is the self-talk of oneness with God, a unity of spirit which transcends all worldly things and gives meaning to our life.

Table 16 Levels of self-talk

I firmly believe that the nature of your self-talk will have a profound impact on the quality of your life. Levels 1 to 3 will hinder your success. Level 4 is a personal choice that will generate rich rewards. Level 5 will have resonance with those of us who aspire to be one with God.

A coaching lifestyle is predicated upon an open-minded, questioning approach to opportunities and challenges.

When things go well we can ask ourselves the question "How did I do that and what have I learnt that I can use in the future?" When things go badly we can use this choice point to pose the question "What have I learnt and what am I going to do differently next time?"

Coaching self-talk could be categorised as 'interrogative' rather than the more 'declarative', positive thinking style of self-talk. Interrogative self-talk elicits answers and within these answers are the options for successfully completing the task. A coaching lifestyle is predicated on the notion that we are more likely to take action when the motivation is intrinsic — 'it is my idea' — rather than extrinsic pressure being brought to bear. Declarative self-talk risks bypassing our emotions, whereas interrogative self-talk unleashes our intrinsic motivation.

'Next time' is a phrase that gladdens my heart! Remember coaching is about now and the future and 'next time'

To Do

Personal investment opportunity

* Take captive every thought. Perhaps every thought is a bit of a tall order, rather concentrate upon identifying your top three positive self-talk scripts and your top three negative ones. Note these in your journal.

* Write the words, see the picture, feel the emotion. Identify one important goal and engage in daily Level 4 self-talk to make it a reality: three stages, write — see — feel.

* Take a gamble on being positive and optimistic. Encourage yourself and others. Choose your words carefully, your subconscious mind is listening!

* Listen and observe the nature of the self-talk scripts operating in members of your family and in your colleagues at work. What do you notice?

provides a fresh opportunity for success. By managing our own self-talk, we are creating the conditions for us to grow and flourish. We can create our own micro-climate that will support growth by using three simple tools in a systematic and disciplined way. They are as follows:

Identify your recurring self-talk scripts. Increase the scripts that serve you and decrease the ones that don't. Use an interrogative approach.

Visualise your goal and engage in Level 4 interrogative self-talk as the foundation upon which to build this creative visualisation.

Make a conscious choice to be optimistic. It is possible to learn to be optimistic, even in the most challenging circumstances.

To remember

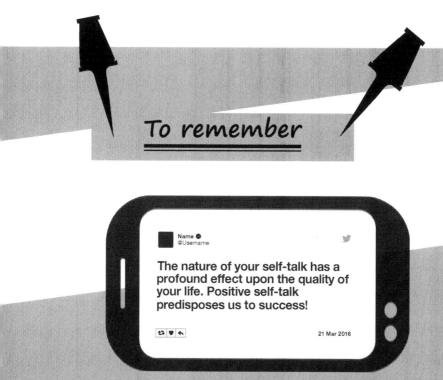

Name
@Username

The nature of your self-talk has a profound effect upon the quality of your life. Positive self-talk predisposes us to success!

21 Mar 2016

LS18 as a tweet

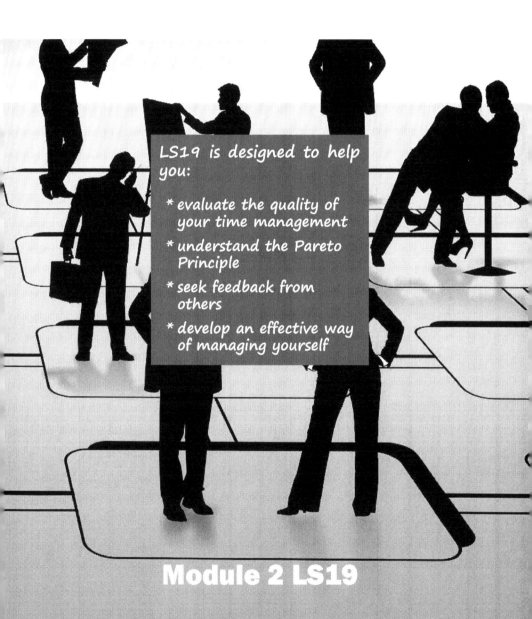

LEARNING STEP 19

How good are you at managing yourself?

LS19 is designed to help you:

* evaluate the quality of your time management
* understand the Pareto Principle
* seek feedback from others
* develop an effective way of managing yourself

Module 2 LS19

LIVING
A
COACHING
LIFESTYLE

Module 2

Module 2: Laying the foundations — developing the core skills

LS20 What have you learned in studying Module 2?

LS19 How good are you at managing yourself?

LS18 What should you say when you talk to yourself?

LS17 What core values support your life's vision?

LS16 Are you committed to developing a coaching lifestyle?

LS15 Who provides you with support and challenge?

LS14 Can you transform plans into action?

LS12 How good is your listening?

LS13 What is the quality of the questions you are posing?

LS11 What is a coaching lifestyle?

How good are you at managing yourself?

Talent without discipline is like an octopus on roller skates. There's plenty of movement, but you never know if it's going to be forward, backwards, or sideways. (H. Jackson Brown, Jr. — American author)

It is necessary to try to surpass one's self always: this occupation ought to last as long as life. (Christina — Queen of Sweden 1632-1654)

It has been said that time management is simply common sense, but not common practice. Effective personal organisation is at the heart of a coaching lifestyle. Time and energy are finite resources that need to be used wisely. You will have a variety of calls on your time and energy and the only person who can manage them is you.

The opening question in LS6 was: *Are you setting the agenda for your own life?* Let us explore this in a bit more detail in relation to your self-management. You will have a variety of SMART goals for different areas of your life; the challenge is to organise yourself in such a way as to make them a reality. So how good is your time management?

Keep a time log for a week and identify exactly where your 168 hours go. Review your time log and look for opportunities to consolidate chunks of discretionary time. The definition of discretionary time is that which is under your personal control and you can choose what you do. Find a time management approach that works for you and use your diary to manage it. I use the *'A' Time* system, developed by James Noon[1].

Noon suggests that you draw up a list of tasks for the day and categorise them in the following way:

A = high value — do today

B = high value — can defer

C = low value — don't do at all

The key to the system is simple, arrange your A tasks in priority order and always do A1 first. The Pareto Principle teaches that 20% of our tasks give us 80% of the results, therefore concentrate on your top A goals. Successful people do not necessarily work harder, but they do concentrate on the important parts of their lives.

The problem is that real life is messy and it is impossible to map out your year, month or even one day without something you haven't planned for happening. The crisis, the emergency, the technological breakdown are all examples of things that need your immediate attention. Noon categorises them as 'X' factors and encourages us to pose the coaching question "Is this urgent event an AX, BX or CX?" If it is an AX, it is both high value and urgent and by definition shoots to the top of the list and needs to be done first.

Time and stress management are the twin pillars of effective self-management. If you do not manage your time well, you are likely to be negatively stressed. If you are stressed you are even more likely to manage your time badly. It is a downward spiral. The good news is that you can coach yourself to effective self-management.

The literature is replete with time and stress management systems and I suggest you find one, or design one, that works for you. Almost all the systems work on the same basic principles:

> *1. Decide on your goals and priorities and write them down.*
>
> *2. Establish a daily 'to do' list that reflects your short, medium and long term goals.*
>
> *3. Use your diary to ensure you are ruthless with time and gracious with people in seeking to achieve your goals.*
>
> *4. Build in review points to assess progress and modify your plans (every two months works for me).*
>
> *5. Seek to achieve a work-life balance that is appropriate to your stage of life and if it is not right at the moment, change it!*

Many General Practices are now offering 'Well Person Checks' and this learning step is your opportunity to devise your own review of the way you are managing yourself. The Jackson Brown quotation above conjures up an imaginative picture of an octopus on roller skates who is expending lots of energy but not going anywhere fast. You may have met people like that. Please don't look in the mirror and see one!

Put aside some time to review your self-management and seek feedback from people you trust both at home and at work. An inability to manage negative stress will have physical and psychological consequences. Increased heart rate and mounting self-doubt are warning signs that need to be attended to. We live in a world of increasing workloads, high demands and role conflict. These are challeng-

To Do

Personal investment opportunity

1. Keep a time log for a week — all seven days (in order to review your work–life balance). Record the key activities of each day and how long you spend on each.

2. Review your log at the end of the week and analyse the patterns you can see emerging.

3. Decide on the changes you would like to make. Start with a modest target of changing the way you spend two hours in your week and reflect on the impact.

4. Devise a stress map. What things are causing you negative stress? Coach yourself using your own variations on the following simple questions:

   » Which of these stressors are under my control and what do I choose to do about them?
   » Which of these stressors can I influence if I choose to? Which of these stressors are out of my control and I just have to accept?
   » In the light of my time log and stress map, what is the quality of my work–life balance?

es that need to be acknowledged and managed.

It is certainly hard to manage anyone else at work, or at home, if you cannot manage yourself first. Indeed, I have the most to gain and the most to lose by the way I manage myself. The quotation from Queen Christina above could be seen as a counsel for constant striving. I prefer to interpret the quotation as a life-long opportunity. I can manage myself better regardless of my age and stage and I can achieve this by **living a coaching lifestyle**!

To remember

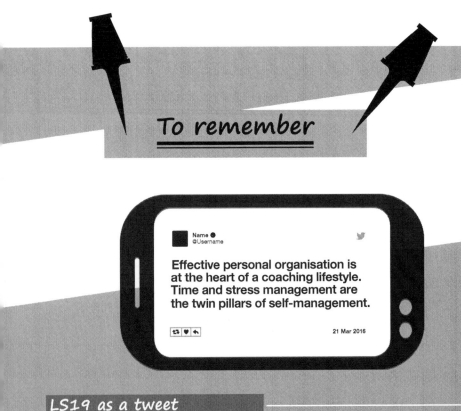

Effective personal organisation is at the heart of a coaching lifestyle. Time and stress management are the twin pillars of self-management.

Name
@Username

21 Mar 2016

LS19 as a tweet

LEARNING STEP 20

What have you learned in studying Module 2?

LS20 is designed to help you:

* pause, draw breath and review your learning again
* review the nine golden threads of Module 2
* answer the review questions
* revisit the objectives of the LaCL Programme

Module 2 LS20

LIVING
A
COACHING
LIFESTYLE

Module 2

Module 2: Laying the foundations — developing the core skills

LS20 What have you learned in studying Module 2?

LS19 How good are you at managing yourself?

LS18 What should you say when you talk to yourself?

LS17 What core values support your life's vision?

LS16 Are you committed to developing a coaching lifestyle?

LS15 Who provides you with support and challenge?

LS14 Can you transform plans into action?

LS12 How good is your listening?

LS13 What is the quality of the questions you are posing?

LS11 What is a coaching lifestyle?

What have you learned in studying Module 2?

> There is no end to education. It is not that you read a book, pass an examination, and finish with education. The whole of life, from the moment you are born to the moment you die, is a process of learning. (Jiddu Krishnamurti — Indian philosopher, speaker and writer)

> Learn as much by writing as by reading. (Lord Acton — English historian and writer)

Congratulations — you are on the twentieth learning step, two thirds of the way through the programme. Pause here for a moment, draw breath, have a look back and review your learning from this second module. You have addressed nine questions so far in this module:

> LS11: What is a coaching lifestyle?

> LS12: How good is your listening?

> LS13: What is the quality of the questions you are posing?

> LS14: Can you transform plans into action?

> LS15: Who provides you with support and challenge?

> LS16: Are you committed to developing a coaching lifestyle?

> LS17: What core values support your life's vision?

> LS18: What should you say when you talk to yourself?

> LS19: How good are you at managing yourself?

This module has been designed to elucidate the components of a coaching lifestyle. Learning steps 11 to 15 highlighted the core skills at the heart of a coaching lifestyle:

» listening for understanding (LS12)

» questioning for depth and breadth (LS13)

» promoting conscious action (LS14)

» engaging the twin pillars of support and challenge (LS15).

The next four learning steps (LS16-19) focussed on how

135

to create the conditions to enable a coaching lifestyle to flourish:

» an analysis of the skill/will matrix (LS16)

» an exploration of the values that underpin your life (LS17)

» the quality of your self-talk (LS18)

» the twin pillars of self-management (LS19).

I have endeavoured to weave nine basic concepts into this second module:

» Dubin's dichotomies

» listening at four levels

» genres of questioning

» action planning

» your 'mastermind group'

» the conditions for developing a coaching lifestyle

» identifying your core values

» the nature of your self-talk

» the quality of your self-management.

These concepts have popped up at various points in the text and personal investment opportunities. I would like to invite you to record your current understanding of each of these golden threads in your journal and I have designed the following questions to focus your thinking.

Reflect on the review questions set out in Table 17 and use your responses as the launch pad for the third module.

The opening quotation in this Learning Step, emphasises that learning is a life-long undertaking, an investment that will continue to produce rich rewards. Lord Acton's quotation is an encouragement to commit your thoughts and reflections to paper, in order to chart your progress towards a coaching lifestyle

As I outlined in the Introduction, my reasons for writing *Living a coaching lifestyle* are summarised in the following four objectives:

» To introduce you to the core skills of coaching.

» To provide you with opportunities to develop these coaching skills, both for your own good and for the good of others.

Review questions

1	How much time and energy have you invested in reflecting on the nine learning steps in Module 2?
2	What does your journal tell you about your learning in Module 2?
3	Where are you in developing a coaching lifestyle, using Dubin's dichotomies as an assessment tool?
4	What have you noticed about the quality of your listening?
5	How good is your questioning technique, and are there any areas for development?
6	How good are you at turning your plans into action?
7	Who is in your mastermind group now? Has it changed?
8	Are you clear about your core values?
9	What is the quality of your self-talk?
10	How good are you at managing yourself?

Table 17 Module 2 review questions

» To encourage you to enjoy change at home and at work.

» To consider living a coaching lifestyle.

As Morecambe and Wise famously used to ask "What do you think of it so far?"

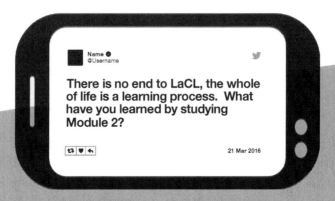

There is no end to LaCL, the whole of life is a learning process. What have you learned by studying Module 2?

21 Mar 2016

LS20 as a tweet

Notes

Notes

What is applied coaching?

LS21 is designed to help you:

* revisit a 'purist' approach to coaching

* recognise two branches in a coaching approach

* make your own judgements about applied coaching

* understand that LaCL is a way of being

Module 3 LS21

LIVING A **COACHING** LIFESTYLE

Module 3

Module 3: Building a coaching lifestyle — applying your learning

LS30 What next?

LS29 What is your definition of living a coaching lifestyle?

LS28 Can coaching boost your most important relationships?

LS27 Can coaching improve friendships?

LS26 Can coaching nurture relentless optimism?

LS24 Can coaching make people really matter at work?

LS25 Can coaching facilitate happiness-centred business?

LS22 Can I utilise a coaching approach at work?

LS23 Can coaching impact an organisational atmosphere?

LS21 What is applied coaching?

What is applied coaching?

Taking personal accountability is a beautiful thing because it gives us complete control over our destinies. (Heather Schuck — American author and 'working mom')

Sir John Whitmore published the first edition of his best-selling book *Coaching for Performance* [1] in 1992. The sub-title of the work is "GROWing People, Performance and Purpose" and thus the GROW model featured in Module 1 (LS5 - LS9) was popularised. My interpretation of the purist approach to coaching espoused in the book can be summarised as having the following characteristics:

» it is non-judgemental

» it is non-directive

» it is client-centred.

This purist approach is built on the notion of a coach supporting the deliberations of a client (coachee) or a client team (coachees). The division of labour could be viewed in the following way.

The role of the coach is to:

» manage the process

» listen well (LS12)

» ask the right questions at the right moment (LS13)

» promote the client taking action (LS14)

» provide support and challenge (LS15)

» if desired keep a written record of the session.

The role of the client is to:

» manage the content

» identify the goal (LS6)

» explore current reality (LS7)

» evaluate the options generated (LS8)

» commit to taking action (LS9)

» live a coaching lifestyle.

I have developed and delivered a variety of coach development programmes over the past fourteen years and the recurring feedback from most apprentice coaches is that 'It is really hard not to tell people what to do'. This is particularly difficult when the coach is a more experienced practitioner in the field of endeavour under discussion. Directive statements masquerading as questions creep into the session — "Could you just...". We spend many of our waking hours telling people what to do. Parents tell their children what to do. Managers tell their staff what to do. Experts are paid to tell clients what to do and so on.

In short, it sounds very simple to develop a coaching approach that is non-judgemental, non-directive and client-centred, but somewhat harder to change a life-time of conditioning. The people who taught me to coach modelled being non-directive by answering every question with a question. For example:

> Neil: "What day is it today?"

> Coach: "What day do you think it is?"

This could become very tedious, in both the home and the workplace, and very time consuming!

During the training phase, the coach trainer has to decide how much direction to give in order to create a positive learning experience for the apprentice coach. The syllabus has to be covered in some creative ways. Indeed, it could be argued that it is impossible for any coach to be completely non-directive as every time we ask a question we change the shape of the client's thinking. When to ask a question and what question to ask are evidence of the coach's judgement calls and undoubtedly have an impact upon the coaching process.

It could also be argued that it is rare for a coach to be completely non-judgemental. The direction of the questioning or an unguarded non-verbal response may shape the conversation. At this point the coaching conversation becomes coach-centred and the coach is shaping the content.

I do believe it is possible to be largely non-judgemental, non-directive and client-centred and I see these elements as a continuum, rather than discrete positions at either end of the scale. The coach makes a judgement call on where

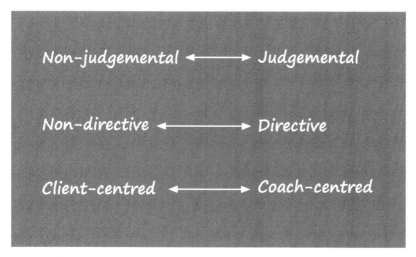

Figure 7 The coaching continuum

to be on each continuum at any given moment (Figure 7).

Coaching is about helping people to design and take action. It is about change. We have covered the basics in the first two modules and hopefully you are now fully aware of the power of coaching. This final module is about applying the principles and practices of coaching in your own life. *Where can a coaching approach serve you?*

This is a branching point. One branch involves employing an external coaching approach with others, the people you work with, the people you socialise with and the people you live with. The other branch embraces the notion of living an internal coaching lifestyle, coaching yourself. These two branches are not mutually exclusive, indeed they are part of the same tree. It is up to you to decide when and how to use your coaching skills. Please note, the old truism definitely applies in relation to the skill of coaching — use it or lose it!

This programme started out as a core primer in the development of the skills required to coach other people (the first branch) and has developed into a way of living your own life (the second branch). The basic skills are the same and I am always attracted to offers of two for the price of one. Living a coaching lifestyle may not be the best way of describing an internal consistency in the way you interact with others and with yourself, but for now it will do.

145

To Do

Personal investment opportunity

When and how will you employ a coaching approach with others:

— at work?

— with acquaintances and friends?

— with family?

What does living a coaching lifestyle mean for you?

What are your personal objectives for this final module?

To remember

Name ✓
@Username

Employ a coaching approach both with others and with yourself. Embody what it means to live a coaching lifestyle.

21 Mar 2016

LS21 as a tweet

In my view, living a coaching lifestyle involves:

» conducting your life in a conscious, mindful state

» nurturing curiosity and investigative awareness

» being open-minded and prepared to seize opportunities when they present themselves

» using coaching skills and techniques in consciously and unconsciously competent ways.

Heather Schuck, in the opening quotation, exhorts us to take 'personal accountability' and describes it as a 'beautiful thing'. This module provides you with the opportunity to decide how to apply the principles and practices of coaching to living and working with others and to your own life. Coaching is about now and the future. The Latin phrase *Carpe diem* literally means 'seize this day'. This imperative is at the heart of a coaching lifestyle.

LEARNING STEP 22

Can I utilise a coaching approach at work?

LS22 is designed to help you:

* decide how you can use coaching at work
* promote a coaching culture to your workplace
* blossom where you are planted
* learn from case-study material

Module 3 LS22

LIVING A COACHING LIFESTYLE

Module 3

LS30 What next?

LS29 What is your definition of living a coaching lifestyle?

LS28 Can coaching boost your most important relationships?

LS27 Can coaching improve friendships?

LS26 Can coaching nurture relentless optimism?

LS24 Can coaching make people really matter at work?

LS25 Can coaching facilitate happiness-centred business?

LS22 Can I utilise a coaching approach at work?

LS23 Can coaching impact an organisational atmosphere?

LS21 What is applied coaching?

Can I utilise a coaching approach at work?

I never cease to be amazed at the power of the coaching process to draw out the skills or talent that was previously hidden within an individual, and which invariably finds a way to solve a problem previously thought unsolvable. (John Russell — American actor and World War Two veteran)

If you are in paid employment you will most likely have a workplace and more importantly a number of people you work with. You may work in a large multi-national company or be part of a small business. You may work in the private sector, the public sector or the charity sector, but the underlying challenge is the same, to be effective and successful. I believe a coaching approach can be utilised in any setting and my challenge to you is to discover how you can increase success in your workplace through coaching in its various forms.

Some organisations have designated internal coaches, other organisations employ external coaches and some organisations have no coaching going on at all. This may reflect the size and scale of the organisation and the priorities established by the people who lead the enterprise. There is an increasing body of research to suggest that coaching organisations are more successful, whether assessed using 'hard' measures (such as bottom line, objective results, staff retention) or 'soft' measures (such as morale, relationships, commitment).

So where do you start? If you are the owner or the most senior person in the enterprise you could decide to introduce a coaching culture and this could be done in a variety of ways:

» invest in a coaching programme for all or some of the workforce

» develop internal coaches to work within the enterprise

» hire external coaches to work with senior staff or designated people

» model a coaching approach on a daily basis.

The options are endless and the judgement call is to know where 'to make the first incision'. These are all top-down approaches that are based on a senior person seeing coaching as a way of moving the organisation forward. A bottom-up approach by contrast relies on individuals within the organisation employing a coaching approach in their work with colleagues and/or customers. This will be a slow-burn strategy, but it will eventually have an impact upon the culture of the organisation.

The importance of organisational culture and the way we work with others has been highlighted by a variety of researchers such as Jim Collins in *Good to Great*[1] and Daniel Goleman in *Emotional Intelligence*[2]. Awareness of others in the workplace is an attitude, a way of being. Furthermore, this practice of emotional intelligence will have a positive impact upon the enterprise's performance. Coaching in the workplace (See LS21 - branch 1) is an organisational behaviour that is predicated upon emotional intelligence. The launch pad of emotional intelligence is intrapersonal intelligence, an understanding of yourself (See LS21 - branch 2).

Coaching could be established in a variety of guises:

A formal coaching programme consisting of one or more of the following:

» one-to-one coaching (using internal or external coaches)

» team coaching (using a coach who is not part of the team)

» line-manager as coach to individual staff members (supervision and performance management)

» line-manager as team coach

» coach development of designated people from within the organisation

An informal programme involving:

» individuals using coaching on an 'ad hoc' basis

» a coaching approach in the way people are led and managed rather than a formal coaching process

» 'grass roots' coaching in the way colleagues work together

» an emphasis upon a people-centred culture

152

My advice is to blossom where you are planted and to

become proactive about how you can employ coaching to enhance the quality of your work. The following short case-study is designed to illustrate the power of coaching in the workplace and to explain why I am so passionate about the power of coaching.

Case-study: Hayes Park School[3]

I was the Head Teacher of Hayes Park for ten years and during that period the school achieved two 'outstanding' Ofsted Inspections and became known as *The Coaching School*. Coaching became a fundamental part of how things were done and had a profound impact upon the quality of both learning and leadership. This is the working definition of 'coaching' that we constructed:

> » it is a process that unlocks a person's potential (child or adult)
>
> » it enables the individual to learn
>
> » it is optimistic about future possibilities
>
> » it is a process that can be used flexibly according to need.

The reason we became passionate about coaching was simple — it worked! It worked for both children and adults and became deeply embedded within the school's culture and our way of doing things. A variety of leadership styles were employed when appropriate, but a coaching approach was our default position. How did we get to this place of 'unconscious competence'?

The 100+ plus staff and 700+ pupils were enthusiastic about learning and the initial impetus was generated by our *Investors in People* Adviser. I attended *The School of Coaching* Programme (see Introduction) and advertised for people to undertake a school-based coach development programme. Twelve coaches started the ball rolling and cohorts of coaches were developed during each of the next five years.

The bare bones of the chronology of our coaching journey are set out below:

> » One-to-one coaching of teachers, using internal coaches
>
> » Associate staff (staff who are not teachers) added to coaching team to work with children and adults
>
> » Team coaching introduced, using a coach from outside the

153

To Do

Personal investment opportunity

Map the business you work in and decide how and where coaching could add value.

Where do you have the ability to employ a coaching approach, either through formal coaching sessions or through the way you work with other people?

Are you being coached? If not, who could you identify as a potential coach that would add value to your work?

To remember

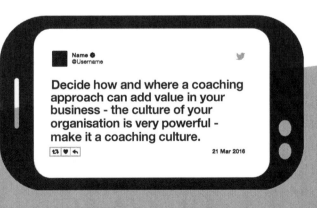

Name
@Username

Decide how and where a coaching approach can add value in your business - the culture of your organisation is very powerful - make it a coaching culture.

21 Mar 2016

LS22 as a tweet

team

» Head Teacher coached by an external coach

» External evaluation of our coaching programme

» Coaching for learning initiatives with the children

» Children coaching other children

» Multiple visitors — international colleagues, researchers and an HMI conducting an 'outstanding practice' visit.

All of these component parts of the coaching programme derived from the belief that learners should take primary responsibility for their own learning and it is the role of the coach to 'ask' and not 'tell'. In retrospect, as the opening quotation asserts, I believe the impact of coaching on those people, children and adults, was profound. Coaching is not a panacea or magic bullet that will solve every problem; rather it is a versatile tool that, used properly, will add enormous value to any organisation — including yours!

Can coaching impact the organisational atmosphere?

LS23 is designed to help you:

* understand social and emotional atmosphere

* tailor strategy to organ- isational readiness

* recognize where your organisation is in its life-cycle

* see that 'coached' work- ers are an asset

Module 3 LS23

LIVING
A
COACHING
LIFESTYLE

Module 3

LS30 What next?

LS29 What is your definition of living a coaching lifestyle?

LS28 Can coaching boost your most important relationships?

LS27 Can coaching improve friendships?

LS26 Can coaching nurture relentless optimism?

LS24 Can coaching make people really matter in work?

LS25 Can coaching facilitate happiness-centred business?

LS22 Can I utilise a coaching approach at work?

LS23 Can coaching impact an organisational atmosphere?

LS21 What is applied coaching?

Can coaching impact the organisational atmosphere?

Coaching is a way of moving another person's thinking forward, it is a way of people actually believing in themselves and finding answers from within. It is a very civilised way of dealing with people. (Susan Dowling — British Head Teacher and Leadership Developer)

I published *Time for Coaching*[1] in spring 2006. This was the fruition of my work as a research associate at the *National College for School Leadership*. This study investigated how and when senior leaders used coaching and the impact that it had on the work of their organisations. Two of the key findings of the study relate to making the workplace a happier environment:

> » Coaching enhances the social and emotional atmosphere of the workplace

> » A coaching strategy should be tailored to suit the organisational readiness of the enterprise, reflecting its unique context and particular circumstances.

The study moved on to evaluate the impact of coaching on the organisations studied. Coaching had encouraged the workforce to be proactive and to take responsibility for their own actions. The adoption of a coaching leadership style by senior leaders had nurtured a collegial approach. In particular, it had:

> » shown people the answers are in their own hands

> » helped people find their own solutions

> » nurtured the growth and development of the workforce

> » become a way of leading and managing

> » reduced confrontation.

At the time, that final bullet point 'reduced confrontation ' surprised me. In the light of mature reflection and further observation, it seems a very obvious outcome of a coaching approach. People are empowered to be creative about finding solutions to their particular challenges and to take the necessary action. This approach builds capacity in the individual, team and whole organisation. It is an investment that will continue to provide future returns. However, a significant initial investment does need to be made at the outset!

Your organisation is unique, it is made up of different people engaged in a variety of roles that are particular to your business. No two organisations are exactly the same and there is no one right way to achieve success, as *Good to Great* (see LS22) illustrated. Nevertheless, the two key findings of my research study do seem to have relevance across most organisations. How do these relate to the organisation that you are part of?

Every organisation is characterised by a particular social and emotional atmosphere. You can usually feel this quite quickly. You walk into a hotel, a surgery or a school and you quickly sense the atmosphere by the way staff relate to you. A warm smile and a friendly word set a positive tone, just as negative body language and lack of acknowledgement make you feel unwelcome. On a day-to-day basis the culture of your organisation and the behaviour of the people you work with have a big impact on how you feel in your workplace.

> How would you describe the social and emotional atmosphere in your workplace? Do other people have a similar view?
>
> How does it feel to work there?
>
> What impact do you have on the atmosphere of the place?
>
> Where can a coaching approach achieve better results in the work you do?

Your organisation is at a particular place in its life-cycle, that reflects its unique context and particular circumstances. The culture in some organisations is more conducive to the introduction of a coaching approach than others, but I believe coaching has a part to play in every enterprise. My repeated challenge to you is to analyse where coaching has a part to play in your workplace.

> What is the nature of your business?
>
> Where is it in its life-cycle - is it developing or decaying?

What is the context your business is operating in?

How would you describe your organisation's state of coaching readiness?

I have worked with a great many enterprises during a long career in leadership development and I am totally confident that coaching can play a part in the further development of any organisation. Many vision statements proudly trumpet that 'people are our key resource' and yet there is little evidence of those organisations actually

To Do

Personal investment opportunity

Look back at your conclusions from the last learning step (LS 22) and invest some additional time in adding to this thinking.

The social and emotional atmosphere of your workplace

1. How would you describe the social and emotional atmosphere in your workplace? (use a scale of 1 to 10 — 1 is very low and 10 is very high)
2. Do other people have a similar view? (ask them)
3. How does it feel to work there?
4. What impact do you have on the atmosphere of the place?
5. Where can a coaching approach achieve better results in the work you do?

The organisational readiness of the enterprise, reflecting its unique context and particular circumstances.

6. What is the nature of your business?
7. Where is it in its life-cycle — is it developing or decaying?
8. What is the context your business is operating in?
9. How would you describe your organisation's state of coaching readiness?

investing in their 'key resources'. In the final analysis, the success of any business depends on recruiting and retaining the right people.

Once the right people have been recruited and inducted effectively, they need to be developed. This is an effort bargain between the organisation and the individual . The investment in individual growth produces a benefit for both parties. Both individual and organisational capacity are increased. One element of this development process should, in my view, be exposure to high quality coaching.

As Susan Dowling's quotation identifies, a 'coached' worker is more likely to show initiative and produce high quality results. They are also more likely to behave in an emotionally intelligent way and build positive relationships with co-workers. In the next learning step we will focus on love in the workplace and the impact this has on performance.

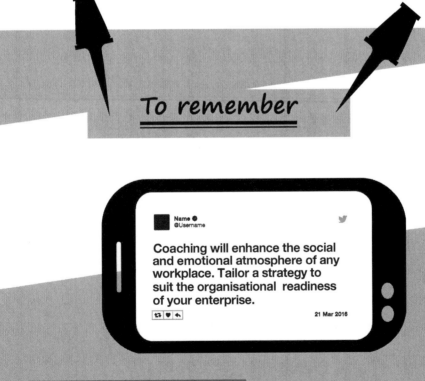

To remember

> **Name** ●
> @Username
>
> Coaching will enhance the social and emotional atmosphere of any workplace. Tailor a strategy to suit the organisational readiness of your enterprise.
>
> 21 Mar 2016

LS23 as a tweet

Can coaching make people really matter at work?

LS24 is designed to help you:

* evaluate the level of love in your workplace

* understand that you can make a difference

* employ left and right brain approaches

* balance procedure and autonomy

Module 3 LS24

LIVING
A
COACHING
LIFESTYLE

Module 3

Module 3: Building a coaching lifestyle — applying your learning

LS30 What next?

LS29 What is your definition of living a coaching lifestyle?

LS28 Can coaching boost your most important relationships?

LS27 Can coaching improve friendships?

LS26 Can coaching nurture relentless optimism?

LS24 Can coaching make people really matter at work?

LS25 Can coaching facilitate happiness-centred business?

LS22 Can I utilise a coaching approach at work?

LS23 Can coaching impact an organisational atmosphere?

LS21 What is applied coaching?

Can coaching make people really matter at work?

The best coaches care about people. They have a sincere interest in people. (Catherine Pilsifer — Canadian author and motivational speaker)

This learning step is dedicated to understanding more of your organisation's character — the level of love in your workplace. When we take a new job we may be unaware of the real nature of the workplace culture we are entering. As time passes it becomes a living reality, but it is not a static phenomenon and is subject to constant modification as the external environment continues to shift and change. For example, the world of education is subject to changing politics, changing economic conditions and differing policy initiatives.

Many people find their workplaces to be increasingly tougher environments, with an inverse relationship between expectations and the resources to meet them. A common business mantra is 'when the going gets tough, the tough get going'. How can a coaching approach flourish in an apparently hostile environment? There are many possible responses to this question, here are four:

» not all workplaces are hostile and over-demanding, some are person-centred and supportive

» each individual can make a difference within their own sphere of influence in an organisation

» the more senior you are, the greater your opportunity to change culture (senior leaders create the 'internal weather')

» in the final analysis you are responsible for your own response to the eco-system of your workplace (see LS 19).

A coaching approach facilitates planned action. It also encourages interpersonal and intra-personal awareness. Roger Harrison, in his seminal book *Organization Culture and Quality of Service*[1], suggests that when the going gets tough we actually need "to do less and feel and imagine more". The sub-title of the book captures the essence of his thinking: *A strategy for releasing love in the workplace.* Many workplaces engender an approach that is competitive and action orientated and encourage left-brain thinking that is analytical, concrete and rational. These can be very positive attributes, but I would suggest they need to be in balance with considerations like co-operation, productive relationships and interdependency. A coaching approach is open to modes of thought and feelings that are right brained: intuitive and amenable to emotional input.

A workplace that reflects a coaching philosophy will have an appropriate balance of standard operating procedures and areas of personal autonomy where people can think for themselves and exercise a degree of personal control. When I have devised a plan of action myself, I am much more likely to implement it. This is at the heart of a coaching approach. This approach, however, is not without risk and responsible managers will need to be confident that giving the workforce appropriate autonomy will not lead to sloppy performance.

Harrison[1] suggests that most organisational cultures don't support the development of the heart and his prescription for nurturing a 'loving' workforce is elaborated:

> » Give credit for their ideas and build on their contributions.

> » Listen to their concerns, hopes, fears, pain: be there when they need an empathetic ear.

> » Treat their feelings as important.

> » Be generous with your trust. Give them the benefit of the doubt.

> » See them as valuable and unique in themselves, and not simply for their contribution to the task.

> » Respond actively to others' needs and concerns; give help and assistance when it is not your job.

> » Look for the good and positive in others, and acknowledge it when you find it.

> » Nurture their growth: teach, support, encourage, smooth the path.

> » Take care of the organisation. Be responsive and responsible to its needs as a living system.

His most telling sentence indicates that in his view developing a 'loving' culture is simple — practise the above nine behaviours. These behaviours, "faithfully, will open the heart of the one who practises, and will warm the heart of those impacted"[1]. They may even work at home!

The idea of releasing *agape* (love) in your workplace may strike an optimistic chord or fill you with deep scepticism, if not anxiety. We are under pressure from every quarter, overbearing leaders, demanding customers and unrealistic expectations — how can releasing 'love' help? Perhaps the word itself does not feel right in a work context. Nevertheless, the underlying principles have undoubted utility and it would be hard to argue against any of the nine behaviours listed.

John Tomsett wrote "This Much I Know About Love Over

To Do

Personal investment opportunity

Look again at Roger Harrison's list of behaviours designed to release love in the workplace.

What is the 'current reality' for each of these nine behaviours in your workplace? Score each one out of ten, one is low, ten is high. That was the easy part of this PIO.

Now bearing in mind that these behaviours "practised faithfully, will open the heart of the one who practises, and will warm the heart of those impacted":

What is the 'current reality' in the way you practise these nine behaviours in your workplace? Score each one out of ten, one is low, ten is high.

And perhaps even more of a challenge (although you may not be like me):

What is the 'current reality' in the way you practise these nine behaviours at home? Score each one out of ten, one is low, ten is high.

Fear"[2] some 28 years after Harrison published "Love in the workplace". Tomsett's book is a compelling account of leading a values-driven school where people matter above all else. His prescription revolves around caring for and developing your workforce and then they will provide a high quality of care to their customers. This is not a mechanistic, manipulative strategy, but rather an approach that consistently puts the needs of people at its centre.

Coaching is a process that has care for people at its heart. The role of owners and leaders of businesses is to create the conditions for people to thrive. People thrive when they are listened to, asked helpful questions at the right moment, encouraged to take action and provided with appropriate support and challenge: coaching!

Catherine Pulsifer believes people can be helped to grow, to develop and to succeed. Her quotation emphasises the belief that the best coaches care about people and the next learning step focuses on the part happiness plays in developing successful workplaces.

To remember

Name ●
@Username

A coaching workplace balances standard operating procedures and areas of personal autonomy where people can exercise a degree of personal control.

21 Mar 2016

LS24 as a tweet

Can coaching facilitate happiness-centred business?

LS25 is designed to help you:

* learn how business, happiness and money can mix

* understand good selfish reasons for action

* focus on quality of service

* become familiar with a 'courtesy system'

Module 3 LS25

LIVING
A
COACHING
LIFESTYLE

Module 3

Module 3: Building a coaching lifestyle — applying your learning

LS30 What next?

LS29 What is your definition of living a coaching lifestyle?

LS28 Can coaching boost your most important relationships?

LS27 Can coaching improve friendships?

LS26 Can coaching nurture relentless optimism?

LS24 Can coaching make people really matter at work?

LS25 Can coaching facilitate happiness-centred business?

LS22 Can I utilise a coaching approach at work?

LS23 Can coaching impact an organisational atmosphere?

LS21 What is applied coaching?

Can coaching facilitate happiness-centred business?

Customers enjoy buying from businesses where the team members are happy. Happy team members tend to be more productive and have a long term commitment to their occupation. (Paddi Lund — Australian dentist, author and motivational speaker)

The bold claim on the cover of *Building the Happiness-centred Business*[1] is that business, happiness and money never mixed until now. This is the story of Paddi Lund and how he transformed his hitherto unhappy Australian dental practice. His contention is that no one can tell you how to be happy at work, it is your personal responsibility. Nevertheless, the environment in which you are operating and your relationships with the people who are working there will have an impact on how you feel.

Most people in full-time employment spend a significant part of their lives in the workplace. As LS23 elaborated, "coaching enhances the social and emotional atmosphere of the workplace". Can coaching increase business success, financial reward and personal and collective happiness? I firmly believe it can and I have had the personal experience of deliberately building a happiness-centred workplace to prove it! Please use the themes of this learning step as a template to review your own workplace (and even your own home).

The basic building blocks of an effective organisation are clear leadership, effective management, common purpose, pleasant environment and effective systems that are fit for purpose. Even so, "the most carefully crafted mission statement will not motivate the team unless they can see some benefit to themselves"[1]. People may have a sincere interest in the needs of their customers, but they also require a good selfish reason for taking action. This could be financial or emotional reward, or the avoidance of punishment.

The quality of service to external customers reflects the way people feel they are being treated by the organisation that employs them. "Unless people are happy within themselves it is hard for them to be consistently pleasant to those whom they serve." [1] The negative power of discourtesy has external ramifications that mirror internal organisational realities. The spirit of the organisation is not encapsulated in the standard operating manual, but rather in the way people treat each other on a day-to-day basis. The transformational process in Paddi Lund's story, and my own experience at Hayes Park School, was in providing motivation to build a courtesy system. The following deceptively simple list of happiness rules reflected a lot of soul-searching, discussion and honest communication for both organisations.

The courtesy system — the happiness centred business[1]

- » Speak very politely using a person's name – 'please' and 'thank you' as a minimum.
- » When you talk about a person who is not present, speak as if they are listening to your conversation. Use the person's name in each sentence in which you refer to them.
- » If you have a problem with someone, talk about the problem only with them and in private.
- » Apologise and make restitution if someone is upset by your actions.
- » Greet and farewell everyone by name, with eye contact and touch.
- » Blame a system not a person.
- » Tell the truth!

The introduction of a courtesy system at Hayes Park was galvanised by engaging the children in developing their own rules. They then designed and made colourful posters for each rule that were strategically displayed around the building. The rules were very simple and captured the essence of how we should interact with one another. Saying 'please' and 'thank-you' is hardly a revolutionary concept, but it can have a revolutionary impact on the nature of a working environment.

The implementation of a courtesy system in both Paddi Lund's dental surgery and a West London school resulted in warmer relationships. When people are polite to us we feel a warmth towards them and feel increasingly good

To Do

Personal investment opportunity

Look at the two following lists below and categorise each item in terms of:

* C (control) — I have some control over this

* I (influence) — I have some influence over this

* NC (no control) — I have no control over this

Identify your top five areas for action in your journal

Happy staff

* Good relationships with other staff

* Good relationships between groups

* Ability to perform at a high standard

* Good relationships with customers

* Clear vision with which you agree

* Sense of being part of a great team with a strong purpose

What staff want of senior managers

* Supportive and approachable

* Interested in all staff

* Fair and friendly

* Open to your input and feedback

* Available and accessible

* Honest in their dealings with you

about ourselves. Behaviour breeds behaviour and positive changes in the social and emotional environment will have discernible benefits for the workforce and the people they serve.

"We spend a large part of our waking hours at work – this makes it important that we have rewarding social contacts in the workplace."[1]This is true for your co-workers as well as you, so you can make a difference by the way you behave. You have more chance of being surrounded by happy people when you are happy yourself. Start by being kind, positive and courteous to people you live and work with.

One of the significant learning points of LS15 is that you are the average of the five people you spend the most time with. You cannot always choose your work colleagues, but you can select your mastermind group. Spend time with happy people and you will have more happiness. Live the change you want to see and be a force for happiness increase. It is a telling commentary on modern working life that anger and cynicism are more acceptable than warmer feelings such as love, humility and kindness.

A coaching approach can address the happiness agenda either directly or obliquely at the individual, team or whole organisational level. Coaching is about now and the future; yesterday is over, let's move on. In my view coaching furnishes an emotional reward as it provides control over what we are going to do next. The courtesy system was at the core of a transition to a happiness-centred environment in the two institutions highlighted — does it have a part to play in your organisation?

Building a happy and productive workplace involves systemising the routine and coaching the exception. Coaching can provide a means to address the 'out of the ordinary', something we haven't done before. It can be the lever for change that helps us move forward , even in challenging and demanding business environments. A final word from Paddi: "For many years I felt inadequate because I found business very difficult. I thought everyone else found it easy." Coaching can address these feelings!

Name ✔
@Username

Behaviour breeds behaviour and positive changes in the social/ emotional atmosphere will have discernible benefits for both workforce and customers.

21 Mar 2016

LS25 as a tweet

Can coaching nurture relentless optimism?

LS26 is designed to help you:

* receive the prescription for a fulfilled life
* learn to be an optimist
* invest in a positive mindset
* retain your optimism even when things go wrong

Module 3 LS26

LIVING
A
COACHING
LIFESTYLE

Module 3

LS30 What next?

LS29 What is your definition of living a coaching lifestyle?

LS28 Can coaching boost your most important relationships?

LS27 Can coaching improve friendships?

LS26 Can coaching nurture relentless optimism?

LS24 Can coaching make people really matter at work?

LS25 Can coaching facilitate happiness-centred business?

LS22 Can I utilise a coaching approach at work?

LS23 Can coaching impact an organisational atmosphere?

LS21 What is applied coaching?

Can coaching nurture relentless optimism?

I am fundamentally an optimist. Whether that comes from nature or nurture, I cannot say. Part of being optimistic is keeping one's head pointed toward the sun, one's feet moving forward. There were many dark moments when my faith in humanity was sorely tested, but I would not and could not give myself up to despair. That way lays defeat and death. (Nelson Mandela — South African President and political activist)

Nelson Mandela continues to be an influential figure, even after his death. This quotation contains his prescription for a fulfilled life — be an optimist, look for the sunshine and keep moving forward. Coaching is about now and the future. There probably will be dark days in your past but the focus is on 'next time'. Mandela suffered imprisonment on Robben Island and yet still managed to retain his relentless optimism — what an example!

Learned Optimism[1] written by Martin Seligman is also inspirational and one of the most influential books I have read. In one way it seems a rather dry tome, written in the language of the psychologist, and yet the message is profound. We can learn to be optimistic. I believe coaching can add rocket fuel to this process both in our personal lives and in our workplaces. This learning step is an exploration of 'how'.

We have a fundamental choice in the way we approach the future. We can be pessimistic and see the future as a threat to be endured. Alternatively, we can see the future as an opportunity and embrace the choices it offers. The conventional wisdom is that success in life results from a combination of talent and desire. On the other hand, failure results from a lack of talent, or desire, or a combination of the two. Seligman's view is that failure could occur when talent and desire are both present, but optimism is missing.

Seligman's theory of success in challenging situations suggests people need three characteristics:

» Aptitude — the talent

» Motivation — the desire

» Optimism — the magic ingredient.

This theory makes interesting reading for the recruitment process. We often appoint people to our organisations on the basis of their aptitude and motivation and fail to explore their predisposition to optimism. Away from work I have become conscious of building friendships with optimistic people. Why? Because spending time with optimistic people helps me be even more optimistic.

There will be occasions when it is very prudent to be pessimistic and to keep your relentless optimism in check. Personally that is in relation to my finances and I want my financial adviser if not to be pessimistic, at the very least to be realistic. Indeed in organisations, it is helpful to have the occasional pessimist who balances the impact of incurable optimists and maybe they will be working in the accounting function. Pessimists are fond of posing 'what if' questions and that keeps corporate feet on the ground.

The case against too much pessimism is easy to make. Pessimism produces inertia in the face of change and ultimately becomes self-fulfilling because pessimistic people don't persevere in the face of challenges. Relentless pessimism eventually leads to poor physical health and depression. Even when things turn out badly and the pessimist was right all the time, they still feel bad. It is hard to win as a pessimist!

The genius of evolution lies in the dynamic tension between optimism and pessimism. That tension enables us to both venture and retrench, in essence to self-correct. The starting point is the direction of your prevailing mindset and Seligman offers us the opportunity to choose an optimistic mindset. In Mandela's terms, to look for the sun and keep moving forward. A coach can help us do that. My question to you is: *Can we learn the skills of an optimistic lifestyle and yet retain a modicum of pessimism for when the situation requires it?*

Achieving an appropriate balance of optimism and pessimism in your life and in your workplace is an ongoing challenge. Balance does not imply equality and I would argue strongly for being optimistic most of the time, both at home and at work. Optimism helps us identify opportunities; pessimism keeps our feet on the ground. A coaching approach to opportunities should embrace positive goal setting, while also taking account of *current reality*.

Learned optimism is a tool to help individuals and organisations achieve the goals they have set. The GROW model sets out to establish a clear goal at the start of the process. The reality stage provides an opportunity to construct an accurate picture of the current state of play, both the optimistic and pessimistic elements. The options that emerge need to be evaluated in the cold light of day, before making a firm commitment at the level of the will.

It is easy to be optimistic when things are going well. It is much harder to retain your relentlessly optimistic approach when things go wrong. This is a wonderful time to examine again the nature of your self-talk (see LS18). Write down the contents of your self-talk when adversity strikes — what are you actually programming into your brain? You have the ability to dispute this negative self-talk and replace it with positive, optimistic scripts.

Your inner dialogue will have both optimistic and pessimistic elements, the challenge is to make most of it optimistic. This is your choice. In order to dispute the negative self-talk successfully, experiment with the following coaching questions:

» What is the evidence for this negative appraisal of the situation?

» Is there another way of looking at this perceived adversity?

» What will be the impact of these circumstances?

» Is it productive to focus on this problem at the moment?

I laid out the behaviours I have committed myself to choose in LS17, they are to:

» manage my own self-talk

» be relentlessly optimistic

» feed my mind through prayer, reflection, reading and coaching

» be a life-long learner

What behaviours are you committed to choosing?

To Do

Personal investment opportunity

Disputing your pessimistic self-talk

Capture the nature of your negative self-talk when things go wrong — write it down and use the four questions set out on the previous page.

How optimistic are you?

Do you believe it is possible to learn to be more optimistic, both at home and at work?

Select one area at home and one at work and choose to be relentlessly optimistic for one month. Note these in your journal.

Remind yourself each day of your areas of optimism.

At the end of the month evaluate how optimistic you have learned to be in these areas.

To remember

LS26 as a tweet

Can coaching improve friendships?

LS27 is designed to help you:

* desire a positive outcome for your client

* employ a growth mind-set

* conceptualise your four circles

* maximise coaching with family and friends

Module 3 LS27

LIVING
A
COACHING
LIFESTYLE

Module 3

LS30 What
next?

LS29 What is your
definition of living a
coaching lifestyle?

LS28 Can coaching
boost your most im-
portant relationships?

LS27 Can coaching
improve friendships?

LS26 Can coaching nurture
relentless optimism?

LS24 Can coaching make
people really matter at
work?

LS25 Can coaching
facilitate happiness-
centred business?

LS22 Can I utilise a
coaching approach
at work?

LS23 Can coaching impact
an organisational atmos-
phere?

LS21 What is applied
coaching?

Can coaching improve friendships?

Coaching is a profession of love. You can't coach people unless you love them. (Eddie Robinson — American football coach)

In LS12, I suggested that you show the quality of care you have for people by the way you listen to them. Eddie Robinson's quotation above may seem a little extreme, depending on your definition of the word 'love'. In LS24 we reflected on love in the workplace[1] and the impact that has on the people who work there. My starting point as a coach will always be that I want a positive outcome for the person I am coaching and that I need to give them my very best. I need to be the best coach I can be.

The mindset of the coach provides an interesting starting point in any coaching scenario. Carol Dweck[2] suggests there are two basic and contrasting mindsets: *fixed* and *growth*. A person with a **fixed** mindset believes that basic attributes like intelligence or talent are fixed traits. They spend their time measuring these existing traits, rather than developing them further. They also believe that talent alone creates success. In my view they are wrong!

People with a **growth** mindset believe their basic abilities can be developed through dedication and hard work. Intelligence and talent are just the starting point, the place where you begin. This mindset creates a love of learning and optimism about the people who are your friends and acquaintances. Growth mindset people take the view that everybody has potential that is waiting to burst forth. This is a great starting point for both formal and informal coaching. In addition, I would rather have friends and acquaintances with this mindset because they will probably be both optimistic and encouraging.

A coaching lifestyle encompasses the way we interact with people. We could draw a socio-gram that represents the people we interact with. A **socio-gram** is a graphic representation of social links that a person has. It is a drawing that plots the structure of interpersonal relations.

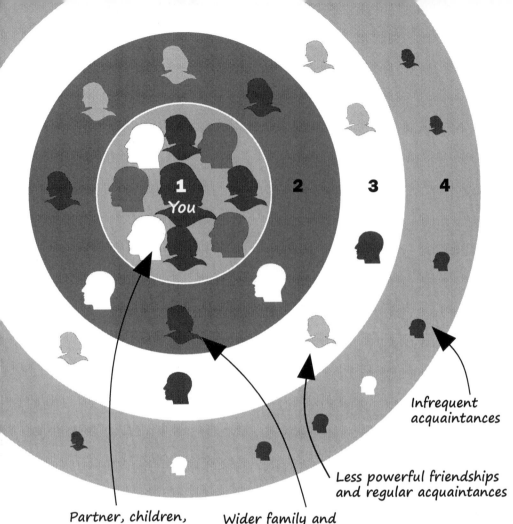

Infrequent acquaintances

Less powerful friendships and regular acquaintances

Partner, children, siblings and parents

Wider family and close friends

Figure 8 A socio-gram of your relationships

Visualise a series of concentric circles with yourself in the middle.

Circle 1, at the centre of the diagram, would be partner, children, siblings and parents.

Circle 2, the next circle out, could contain wider family and close friends.

Circle 3 might contain less powerful friendships and regular acquaintances.

Circle 4 will be larger still and will identify people with whom you have a less strong relationship and meet infrequently.

To Do

Personal investment opportunity

1. Draw a socio-gram — use concentric circles or any other model that helps you map your social relationships.

What do you notice about the inhabitants of:

* circle 1

* circle 2

* circle 3

* circle 4

2. Reflect on how you might use a coaching approach and the core skills of coaching in your relationships with the people in your four circles. Note your conclusions in your journal.

To remember

Name
@Username

Invest in a growth mindset that creates a love of learning and optimism about the people who are your friends and acquaintances.

21 Mar 2016

LS27 as a tweet

You decide on the criteria for allocating individuals to particular circles. The likelihood is that you spend more time and energy on the people in the inner circles. For the purpose of this learning step, I am inviting you to reflect on the nature of your relationships in circles 2, 3 and 4. Can a coaching approach enhance the quality of your relationships with friends and acquaintances? I am beginning to believe it can.

The core skills at the heart of a coaching lifestyle (see LS11) are:

> » listening for understanding
> » questioning for depth and breadth
> » promoting conscious action
> » engaging with the twin pillars of support and challenge.

If we soften the words but retain the underlying philosophy, we could re-designate these core skills as:

> » showing our quality of care for people by the way we listen to them
> » taking an interest in what is going on in their world and asking helpful questions to support and challenge their thinking
> » helping them sort out what they are going to do next over a cup of tea or a glass of wine
> » displaying an appropriate balance of unconditional support and intellectual challenge.

The Oxford Dictionary definition of **friend** is "a person with whom one enjoys mutual affection and regard". The same dictionary defines **acquaintance** as "a person one knows slightly". In the concentric circles model above, some acquaintances develop into friends in circle 3. How does that happen for you? I am attracted to people who have a good sense of humour and understand the unspoken law of reciprocity and are 'conversationally generous'. I ask you a question and listen to your answer with genuine interest and then you return the compliment by doing the same. We demonstrate a level of mutual interest and concern for the feelings of the other. This is the ballroom dance of social relationship building.

Deconstructed in this way, friendship appears cold and calculating and in reality few of us analyse the process of friendship-making at the conscious level. Nevertheless, I am convinced that asking people about their lives and views of the world and listening carefully to their answers are powerful building blocks in the social process. Have a look at the people who populate circle 2 and circle 3 in your life. Are there any recurring themes in the way they interact with you? What do they have to do to move from circle 3 to circle 2?

Pure coaching is non-directive, non-judgemental and client-centred. Does it share any common features with friendship? We can choose our behaviour to build friendship or to bolster social distance. Figure 9 shows a continuum that provides a way of conceptualising how directive we choose to be in the mode of behaviour we adopt.

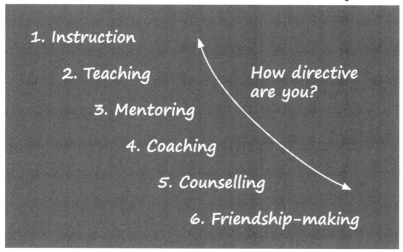

Figure 9 The directive continuum

Both coaching and friendship are a long way from instruction and teaching in terms of how directive you are. Few people set out to build friendships in order to practise their coaching skills and that is not the intention of this learning step. Rather I am inviting you to reflect on how you might use a coaching approach and the core skills of coaching to build positive relationships with the people in your inner and even outer circles. I love the people who are in my circle 1 and in the next step we will explore the utility of developing a coaching lifestyle with those nearest and dearest to us.

Can coaching boost your most important relationships?

LS28 is designed to help you:

* reflect on where you invest time and energy
* review how you listen to your inner circle
* ask the best question at the opportune moment
* decide when to tell and when to ask

Module 3 LS28

LIVING
A
COACHING
LIFESTYLE

Module 3

LS30 What next?

LS29 What is your definition of living a coaching lifestyle?

LS28 Can coaching boost your most important relationships?

LS27 Can coaching improve friendships?

LS26 Can coaching nurture relentless optimism?

LS24 Can coaching make people really matter at work?

LS25 Can coaching facilitate happiness-centred business?

LS22 Can I utilise a coaching approach at work?

LS23 Can coaching impact an organisational atmosphere?

LS21 What is applied coaching?

Can coaching boost your most important relationships?

> No matter what you've done for yourself or for humanity, if you can't look back on having given love and attention to your own family, what have you really accomplished? (Elbert Hubbard — American writer, publisher and philosopher)

LS27 defined the inner circle of your life as partner, children, siblings and parents. I have no living siblings or parents, but I do have a wife, three children and seven grandchildren. These people truly are at the centre of my life. My question to myself is: *Do I make that a conscious current reality for them and for myself?* This question leads to reflections about the way I invest my time and energy. It also causes me to reflect on the goals and the priorities I establish, both consciously and unconsciously. Who are the people in your inner circle?

We learn a lot from our parents and as we grow older we begin to look more and more like them — it is uncanny. We probably spend most time with our partner and the obvious difference between partner and blood relatives is that you chose her or him! Hopefully, our children are the greatest gift in life and often the greatest challenge. It is said that blood is thicker than water and one would hope to always be in a positive relationship with our children. We have a plaque on our kitchen wall that asserts 'Grandchildren are the crowning glory of the aged'. I believe that statement to be true!

We show the quality of our care for people by the way we listen to them (LS12). Listening is a vital life skill. It is at the heart of almost everything we do. We spend a large part of our waking hours engaged in the business of listening, either to others or to ourselves. It is the first key element of a coaching lifestyle because it creates an environment for change. At the very least, listening can be seen as the highest form of courtesy as you are conferring your attention and interest on the speaker. Surely the people in our inner circle deserve this level of attention.

The quality of our listening ebbs and flows for a variety of reasons, such as our level of tiredness, the nature of the topic and our relationship with the speaker. The judgement call is to decide when to unleash our highest level listening in order to make sense of the world, plan the future or build positive family relationships. The quality of our listening changes with the amount of focussed effort we direct towards what we are listening to. It is a tiring activity and so learning where to invest our 'best listening' in our family will pay dividends.

The notion of employing different 'levels of listening' provides a useful working model in family situations (LS12).

Level	Listening quality	Description
1	Surface listening	Listening from habit, meaningless chatter and social 'buzz' (closed mind)
2	Factual listening	Paying attention and noticing differences that could be useful or important later (open mind)
3	Empathetic listening	Connecting at an emotional level and seeing the world through the eyes of the speaker (open heart)
4	Generative listening	Ability to connect with an emerging future and the shifting identity of the speaker (open will)

Table 18 Listening quality

A coaching lifestyle is characterised by a questioning approach to all we think and do. As we rehearsed in LS13, we listen in order to understand and make sense of what is going on. Asking the right question at the right moment often provides the key to unlocking a complex situation. Indeed, framing a well-chosen question will help to:

» clarify the goal

» explore current thinking and feeling

» generate a breadth and depth of options

» build commitment to taking action

» give focus to the inner circle dialogue.

Young children ask question after question and this is how they learn about themselves and the world around them. As adults we can choose to perpetuate this enquiring approach and to consciously develop our questioning technique in order to support and challenge the people in our inner circle. As a parent or grandparent we make a judgement call about when to 'tell' and when to 'ask'. I believe coaching can enhance family life by asking good questions at the opportune moment.

The twin themes of effective coaching — 'raising awareness' and 'taking responsibility for the action' — are very important in family interactions. A matriarchal or patriarchal 'telling' approach may occasionally be appropriate, but for the most part I am committed to a coaching, questioning approach. My place on the following continuum (Figure 10) will reflect the age and stage of the person I am interacting with and what is appropriate.

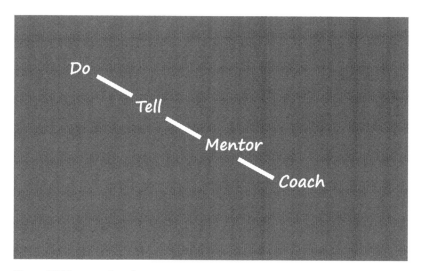

Figure 10 Where am I on the continuum?

DO — TELL— MENTOR — COACH.

The cut and thrust of family life is helped by seeing things from the other person's position. The three perceptual positions in neuro-linguistic programming are very helpful in this context:

195

First Position: seeing, hearing and feeling the situation through your own eyes, ears and feelings. You think in terms of what is important to you, what you want to achieve.

Second Position: stepping into the shoes of the other person and experiencing (seeing, hearing and feeling) the situation as if you were them. You think in terms of how this situation would appear or be interpreted by that other person — in my case, wife, child or grandchild.

Third Position: standing back from a situation and experiencing it as if you were a detached observer. You think in terms of what opinion, observations or advice would someone offer who is not involved.

The key challenge in adopting a coaching approach with family members is our ability to be non-directive, non-judgmental and client-centred. We care passionately about these people and may often feel we know best! Nevertheless, a coaching approach can produce a better outcome and a greater likelihood of implementation than the best-intentioned advice. You decide!

It is undoubtedly the case that we see our own worst faults in those nearest and dearest to us and I think at the very least it is important that we provide them with the opportunity to be different. How can we help them grow?

> » Listen passionately as a means of releasing love in the relationship
>
> » Ask coaching questions to deepen their thinking
>
> » Encourage them to take responsibility for choosing a course of action
>
> » Provide either support or challenge, according to their needs and the needs of the situation.

Inner circle coaching will demonstrate the love of the giver and warm the heart of the receiver. Like Elbert Hubbard, I want to be able to look back on family life and honestly say that I gave each one my profound love and undivided attention.

To Do

Personal investment opportunity

Look at your inner circle and make an honest appraisal of your relationship with close family members, for example:

* your partner

* your children

* your grandchildren

* your siblings

* your parents

When and where might it be appropriate to adopt a coaching approach?

Find an opportunity to make a coaching investment with each person in your inner circle and record the outcomes in your learning journal.

To remember

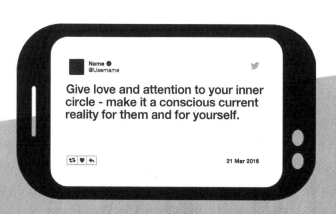

Name
@Username

Give love and attention to your inner circle - make it a conscious current reality for them and for yourself.

21 Mar 2016

LS28 as a tweet

What is your definition of living a coaching lifestyle?

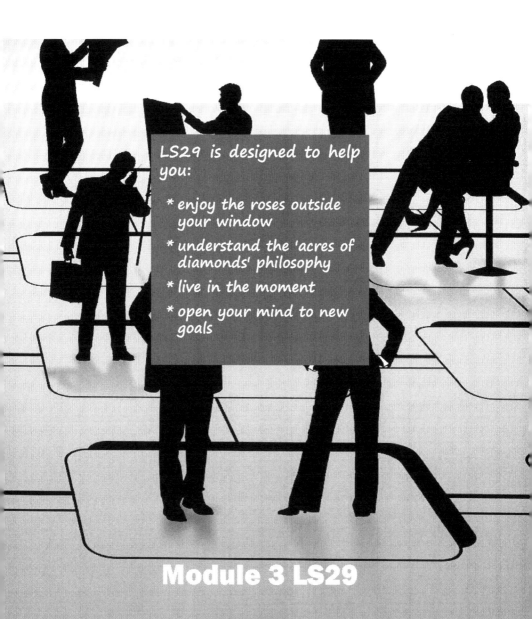

LS29 is designed to help you:

* enjoy the roses outside your window
* understand the 'acres of diamonds' philosophy
* live in the moment
* open your mind to new goals

LIVING A **COACHING** LIFESTYLE

Module 3

LS30 What next?

LS29 What is your definition of living a coaching lifestyle?

LS28 Can coaching boost your most important relationships?

LS27 Can coaching improve friendships?

LS26 Can coaching nurture relentless optimism?

LS24 Can coaching make people really matter at work?

LS25 Can coaching facilitate happiness-centred business?

LS22 Can I utilise a coaching approach at work?

LS23 Can coaching impact an organisational atmosphere?

LS21 What is applied coaching?

What is your definition of living a coaching lifestyle?

One of the most tragic things I know about human nature is that we all tend to put off living. We are all dreaming of some magical rose garden over the horizon, instead of enjoying the roses that are blooming outside our windows today. (Dale Carnegie — American author and motivational speaker)

The **Living a coaching lifestyle** programme has been designed to challenge you to enjoy the roses that are blooming outside your window now. You are the architect of your own destiny and you can choose the lifestyle you live. As I have already said in earlier learning steps, the days are long, but the time is short. I hope you have a treasure trove of reflections in your learning journal and that you are turning this thinking into concrete action.

I would like to share with you a summarised version of one of my favourite stories: *Acres of diamonds*[1]. A young South African farmer becomes obsessed with finding the diamond that will make him rich beyond his wildest dreams. He sells the family farm and uses the proceeds to fund his to search for the elusive diamond. After years of struggle and disappointment, his money has run out and he is so desperate that he drowns himself in the nearest river.

Meanwhile back at the farm, the young couple who have purchased the place have a knowledgeable guest come to supper. His eye is attracted to a large shiny stone on their mantelpiece and he innocently asks them where it came from. They reply that it came from their brook and there are acres of these stones. Of course, it turns out to be the biggest diamond in the world and they are the owners of acres of diamonds, thus the title of the story.

The moral of the tale is that the diamonds are already under your feet, or if you prefer Carnegie's rose metaphor, they are already blooming outside your window. The challenge is to recognise them. This is where the reticular activating system comes into play and you literally need to open your eyes. This is LS29, the penultimate learning step. I would like to revisit LS11 and pose the question once again: *What is a coaching lifestyle?*

In LS11, I proposed the notion that a coaching lifestyle involves:

» conducting your life in a conscious, mindful state

» nurturing curiosity and investigative awareness

» being open-minded and prepared to seize opportunities when they present themselves

» using coaching skills and techniques in consciously and unconsciously competent ways.

Mindfulness is becoming a very popular movement that emphasises focusing one's awareness on the present moment. This involves calmly acknowledging and accepting feelings, thoughts and bodily sensations. Curiosity is the launch pad for investigation and discovery. Opportunities will present themselves, the clever bit is to recognise them. Once they have been recognised, a coaching approach will help us to maximise them, either consciously or unconsciously.

As you have worked your way through this programme you will have come to your own conclusions about the utility and application of coaching principles and practices. You have the rest of your life to experiment with ways of harnessing your learning and building a positive future. This is not a selfish undertaking, but rather a way of investing in yourself for the benefit of the people you live and work with. The past is over, it is about now and the future.

Whatever your history, you have the resources to reshape your life and the world around you for the better. Coaching opens the mind to new goals and gives us options about how to move forward. Opportunities are all around us, just like the diamonds in the story. You simply have to open your RAS to see them. It is then about your level of commitment to action. You can turn these opportunities into realities by fully committing yourself at the level of the will.

Barbara Fredrickson sums it up beautifully when she sug-

To Do

Personal investment opportunity

What diamonds are under your feet? What roses are blooming under your window?

What is preventing you from mining these diamonds or harvesting these roses?

Construct your own definition of a coaching lifestyle, based on the reflections you have captured in your reflective learning log.

To remember

Name
@Username

You are the architect of your own destiny. You can choose the lifestyle you live - discover the diamonds under your feet!

21 Mar 2016

LS29 as a tweet

gests: "Positivity — whether it blooms as joy, serenity, or any other hue on your positivity palette — literally gives you a new outlook on life... Positivity broadens our minds and expands our range of vision."[2] It also makes us more fun to be with! We have a daily choice — to be pessimistic and focus on what can go wrong, or to be optimistic and commit to what we can make go right.

As Winston Churchill said "No boy or girl should ever be disheartened by lack of success in their youth but should diligently and faithfully continue to persevere and make up for lost time."[3] Success is not final, failure is not fatal: it is courage to continue that counts. Don't put off living your own coaching lifestyle!

What next?

LS30 is designed to help you:

* celebrate the completion of the programme

* decide whether you are brave enough to be a butterfly

* live a life congruent with your core values

* review your learning from LaCL

Module 3 LS30

LIVING
A
COACHING
LIFESTYLE

Module 3

Module 3: Building a coaching lifestyle — applying your learning

LS30
What next?

LS29 What is your
definition of living a
coaching lifestyle?

LS28 Can coaching
boost your most im-
portant relationships?

LS27 Can coaching
improve friendships?

LS26 Can coaching nurture
relentless optimism?

LS24 Can coaching make
people really matter at
work?

LS25 Can coaching
facilitate happiness-
centred business?

LS22 Can I utilise a
coaching approach
at work?

LS23 Can coaching impact
an organisational atmos-
phere?

LS21 What is applied
coaching?

What next?

How does one become a butterfly? You must want to fly so much that you are willing to give up being a caterpillar. (Trina Paulus — American author and organic farmer)

To be yourself in a world that is constantly trying to make you something else is the greatest accomplishment. (Ralph Waldo Emerson — American essayist, lecturer and poet)

Congratulations! You have reached the last learning step in '**Living a coaching lifestyle**'!

I was recently sent a card and advised to put it next to my shaving mirror. The card proclaims:

"Take a moment every morning when you look in the mirror to remind yourself that today is going to be a truly great day."

One thing is for certain, we will only have this day once. I suggest to you that it obliges us to make the most of each day. Mine the diamonds or cut the roses, choose whatever metaphor stimulates your thinking.

This final module has focused upon applied coaching and learning steps LS21 to LS29 have addressed living a coaching lifestyle both in the workplace and at home. This module poses a series of questions concerning the application of coaching to your life:

» Can coaching make a difference in your workplace?

» Can coaching nurture happiness and relentless optimism?

» Can coaching enhance your relationships with friends and acquaintances?

» Can coaching add value to your most important relationships?

As your coach, it is my great pleasure to pose these questions. As the person making the changes, your challenge is to find the answers that work for you. You have already accepted this challenge and the good news is that you have the rest of your life to refine the way you live your own unique coaching lifestyle. Trina Paulus is an author and environmentalist and the quotation above addresses the question of whether we really want to be different. You may be very satisfied with many areas of your life and it would seem eminently sensible to keep doing what you are doing. Look again at the *Wheel of Life* in LS2. Where you are not satisfied, try something different. I believe commitment at the level of the will (the W in the GROW model) is the key to successful change. Do you want to be a butterfly in these areas or do you prefer to keep moaning about being a caterpillar? Take action.

You are now in possession of all the basic tools that will enable you to live a coaching lifestyle. You have explored the GROW model in great detail and you are familiar with the four stages (LS5):

> » G — goal
>
> » R — current reality
>
> » O — options
>
> » W — will

You have also developed the four core skills at the heart of a coaching lifestyle:

> » listening for understanding
>
> » questioning for depth and breadth
>
> » promoting conscious action
>
> » engaging with the twin pillars of support and challenge.

Look back through your learning journal and reflect on what you have learnt. Learning is a very satisfying undertaking. It is also the launch pad for new action. For the very last time, if you always do what you have always done, you will always get what you have always got! The answer is blindingly obvious — do something different.

> *Reflect upon your DO — HAVE — BE:*
>
> *What do you DO?*
>
> *In order to HAVE?*
>
> *Who do you want to BE?*

We often expend a lot of energy trying to please the people we work with or the people we live with. This is an honourable undertaking that needs to balanced with our own goals and intentions. Investing in ourselves is not a

To Do

Personal investment opportunity

What next?

Read through your learning journal and highlight the things that jump out at you. This is your agenda for change. You have the rest of your life to address the issues you have identified.

Choose your most pressing issue or greatest opportunity and start today!

Living a coaching lifestyle (LaCL) final review

What have you learned about:

» listening for understanding
» questioning for depth and breadth
» promoting conscious action
» engaging with the twin pillars of support and challenge?
» How are you using the GROW model in your work and home life?
» What does living a coaching lifestyle mean for you?
» Has the programme modified the way you do things?

Programme review

» What have you enjoyed most about the programme?
» What have you enjoyed least about the programme?
» Have you any suggestions about how the programme can be improved?

Commitments

» As a result of investing in this programme I will...
» As a result of investing in this programme I will no longer...
» My top priority now is to...

selfish activity. Indeed, it could be seen as an altruistic undertaking as we are more productive and more fun to be around.

Life is a fascinating journey and is to be lived to the full. My personal prescription is to live a life that is congruent with my core values. These values modify and become nuanced over time. Nevertheless, they provide the bedrock for decisions about my lifestyle. We make decisions daily about how we will invest our time and energy. I believe these decisions will be enhanced by applying the skills and techniques of coaching.

Ralph Waldo Emerson was an American essayist, lecturer and poet. The quotation above captures my motivation to be the person I want to be. When you let go of the pressure to be something you are not, you create space for new opportunities. New opportunities present themselves and provided the RAS is open for business, you can seize them with both hands.

To remember

Name
@Username

Congratulations! You have finished the programme - use what you have to live your very own coaching lifestyle.

21 Mar 2016

LS30 as a tweet

Your challenge now is to maximise the power of the investment you have made in this programme. Remember the famous maxim — The more I practise the luckier I get. I beg you not to consign your learning journal to a dusty cupboard or an unopened computer file. Harvest your learning and use it to inform the way you conduct the rest of your life. Live your own coaching lifestyle from today onwards!

Notes	

Notes

Endnote references

LS5

1. Alexander, G & Renshaw, B (2005) *Supercoaching*

LS8

1. Maltz, M (1960) *Psycho-cybernetics*

LS16

1. Whitmore, J (2002) *Coaching for performance*

LS17

1. Seligman, M. (2011) *Flourish* Nicholas Brealey

LS18

1. Helmstetter, S (1986) *What to say when you talk to yourself*

LS19

1. Noon, J (1985) *'A' Time: The busy manager's action plan for effective self-management*

LS22

1. Collins, J C (2001) *Good to Great*
2. Goleman, D (1995) *Emotional Intelligence*
3. Suggett, E N (2012) "Coaching in Primary Schools: A Case-study" In: van Niewerburgh, C (ed.) *Coaching in Education*

LS23

1. Suggett, E N (2006) *Time for Coaching* National College for School Leadership Research Associate Report

LS24

1. Harrison, R (1987) *Organization Culture and Quality of Service*
2. Tomsett, J (2015) *This Much I Know About Love Over Fear*

LS25

1. Lund, P (1994) *Building the happiness-centred business*

LS26

1. Seligman, M (1990) *Learned Optimism*
2. Seligman, M (2011) *Flourish* (I haven't quoted directly from this book, but I would recommend it as a great adjunct to LS26)

LS27

1. Harrison, R (1987) *Organization Culture and Quality of Service*
2. Dweck, C (2006) *Mindset: How You Can Fulfil Your Potential*

LS29

1. Allen, J (1890) *Acres of diamonds*
2. Fredrickson, B (2009) *Positivity*
3. Churchill, W (1946) Speech, University of Miami

Quotation sources

Introduction (Jim Rohn - goodreads.com); **LS1** (Lao Tzu - quotationspage.com, Joe Girard - quotationsbook.com); **LS2** (J.K Rowling - brainyquote.com); **LS3** (Galileo - brainyquote.com); **LS4** (Linda Nilson - crla.net); **LS5** (Graham Alexander - Alexander, G. & Renshaw, B. (2005) *Supercoaching)*; **LS6** (Waitley, D. (1995) *Empires of the Mind);* **LS7** (F Nietzche - wikiquote.org); **LS8** (William Fullbright - quotes.net); **LS9** (Jason Vale - goodreads.com); **LS10** (Chinese Proverb - quotegarden.com, C. JoyBell C. - goodreads.com); **LS11** (H Jackson-Brown - (2012) *Life's Little Instruction Book);* **LS12** (Barbara Ward - (1985) Lecture to Hillingdon Head Teachers); **LS13** (Naguib Mahfouz - brainyquote.com); **LS14** (Erin Cummings - brainyquote.com); **LS15** (Jim Rohn - goodreads.com); **LS16** (John Whitmore - (2002) *Coaching for Performance);* **LS17** (Danny Meyer - inc.com); **LS18** (Helmstetter, S. (1986) *What To Say When You Talk To Yourself);* **LS19** (H Jackson-Brown - (2012) *Life's Little Instruction Book);* **LS20** (Jiddu Krishnamurti - thinkexist.com); **LS21** (Heather Schuck - goodreads.com); **LS22** (John Russell coachingtosuccess.co.uk); **LS23** (Suggett, E. N. (2006) *Time for Coaching NCSL);* **LS24** (Catherine Pulsifer - wow4u.com); **LS25** (Lund, P. (1994) *Building The Happiness-centred Business);* **LS26** (Nelson Mandela - goodreads.com); **LS27** (Eddie Robinson - philosiblog.com); **LS28** (Elbert Hubbard - brainyquote.com); **LS29** (Dale Carnegie - brainyquote.com); **LS30** (Trina Paulus - goodreads.com, Ralph Waldo Emerson - quotationsbook.com)

Further reading

These books have shaped my thinking.

Coaching

Alexander, G. & Renshaw, B. (2005) *Supercoaching* Random House

Bacon, T. & Spear, K. (2003) *Adaptive Coaching* Davies-Black

Blakey, J. & Day, I. (2012) *Challenging Coaching* Nicholas Brealey

Downey, M. (1999) *Effective Coaching* Orion Business

Biswas-Diener, R. & Dean, B. (2007) *Positive Psychology Coaching* John Wiley

Neale, S. Spencer Arnell, L. & Wilson, L. (2009) *Emotional Intelligence Coaching* Kogan Page

Scoular, A. (2011) *Business Coaching* Prentice Hall

Stanier, M. B. (2016) *The Coaching Habit* Box of Crayons Press

Van Nieuwerburgh, C (2012) *Coaching in Education* Karnac Books

Stoltzfus, T. (2005) *Leadership Coaching* Coach 22

Taylor, D. (2007) *The Naked Coach* Capstone

Whitmore, J. (2002) *Coaching for Performance* Nicholas Brealey

General

Brown, B. (2010) *The Gifts of Imperfection* Hazelden

Brown, B. (2012) *Daring Greatly* Penguin Random House

Cameron, J. (1994) *The Artist's Way* Souvenir Press

Cashman, C. (2008) *Leadership From The Inside Out* Berret-Koehler

Dweck, C (2006) *Mindset: How You Can Fulfil Your Potential* Constable & Robinson

Dyer, W. (2010) *The Power of Intention* Hay House

Fredrickson, B. (2009) *Positivity* Oneworld Publications

Gallwey, T. (1974) *The Inner Game of Tennis* Pan

Jackson-Brown, H. (2012) *Life's Little Instruction Book* Thomas Nelson

Harrison, R. (1987) *Organization Culture and Quality of Service* AMED

Helmstetter, S. (1986) *What To Say When You Talk To Yourself* Thorsons

Lund, P. (1994) *Building The Happiness-centred Business* Solutions Press

Maltz, M. (1960) *Psycho-cybernetics* Prentice-Hall

Noon, J. (1985) *A Time* Chapman & Hall

Peters, S. (2012) *The Chimp Paradox* Vermilion

Ratcliffe, S (2012) *Leadership Plain and Simple* FT Publishing

Seldon, A (2016) *Beyond Happiness* Yellow Kite

Seligman, M. (1990) *Learned Optimism* Random House

Seligman, M. (2011) *Flourish* Nicholas Brealey

Suggett, E. N. (2006) *Time for Coaching* NCSL

Syed, M. (2015) *Black Box Thinking* John Murray Publishers

Tomsett, J. (2015) *This Much I Know About Love Over Fear* Crown House

Waitley, D. (1995) *Empires of the Mind* Nicholas Brealey

Index

Symbols

4Fs model 56, 57

A

Acres of diamonds 201, 213
Action (in GROW model) 44, 45, 65, 66, 67, 68, 69, 85, 124, 159, 165, 166, 168, 169, 171, 173, 188, 201, 202
Acton, Lord 135, 136
Agape 167
Alexander, Graham 43, 213, 214, 215
'A' Time 129, 213
Authentic Happiness 116

B

'Being' (goals) 41, 47, 50, 51, 52

C

Carnegie, Dale 201, 214
Christina, Queen of Sweden 129, 132
Churchill, Winston 204, 213
C. JoyBell C. 73, 214
Coaching continuum 145
Coaching for Performance 112, 143, 214, 215
Coaching lifestyle, Living a 6, 11, 12, 13, 15, 19, 20, 21, 25, 31, 32, 33, 34, 41, 42, 43, 73, 75, 77, 79, 80, 81, 82, 85, 91, 94, 97, 103, 104, 107, 109, 110, 111, 116, 129, 132, 135, 136, 137, 143, 145, 146, 147, 193, 194, 199, 201, 202, 203, 204, 207, 208, 209, 211
Collins, Jim 152, 213
Courtesy system 169, 172, 174
Cummings, Erin 97, 98, 100, 214
Current reality (in GROW model) 19, 44, 45, 50, 53, 55, 56, 57, 58, 87, 208

D

Directive continuum 189
'Doing' (goals) 50, 51
Dowling, Susan 159, 162
Dubin's dichotomies 81, 82, 121, 136, 137

Dweck, Carol 185, 213, 215

E

Einstein, Albert 64
Emerson, Ralph Waldo 207, 210, 214
Emotional Intelligence 213, 215

F

Family 12, 13, 19, 33, 80, 87, 122, 146, 183, 186, 193, 194, 195, 196, 197, 201
Flourish 116, 213, 215
Fredrickson, Barbara 202, 213, 215
Fulbright, William 61, 62

G

Galileo 31, 32, 37, 214
Gandhi 117
Girard, Joe 19, 20, 214
Goal (in GROW model) 43, 44, 45, 49, 50, 52, 55, 61, 62, 63, 67, 68, 124, 125, 181
Goal-setting 44, 50
Goleman, Daniel 152, 213
Good to Great 160, 213
GROW 13, 41, 43, 45, 49, 55, 56, 57, 61, 67, 74, 93, 110, 143, 181, 208, 209
Growth mindset 183, 185

H

Happiness 169, 170, 171, 172, 174
Harrison, Roger 165, 167, 168, 213, 215
Hayes Park (School) 2, 5, 153, 172
Helmstetter, Shad 121, 213, 214, 215
Hubbard, Elbert 193, 196, 214

J

Jackson Brown, Jr., H. 129

K

Krishnamurti, Jiddu 135, 214

L

LaCL See also *Coaching lifestyle, Living*

a 11, 17, 19, 25, 31, 59, 71, 107, 133, 141, 205, 209

Lao Tzu 19, 21, 214

Learned Optimism 213, 215

Listening 80, 81, 85, 97, 122, 123, 193, 194

Lund, Paddi 171, 172, 213, 214, 215

M

Mahfouz, Naguib 91, 93, 214

Maltz, Maxwell 62, 213, 215

Mandela, Nelson 69, 179, 180, 214

Mastermind group 68, 74, 81, 101, 103, 104, 105, 136, 137, 174

Meyer, Danny 115, 214

Mindfulness 202

Mother Teresa 69

N

National College for School Leadership 159, 213

Neuro-linguistic programming 195

Nietzsche, Friedrich 55, 57

Nilson, Linda B. 37, 39, 214

Noon, James 129, 130, 213, 215

O

Optimism 177, 179, 180, 181, 182, 185

Options (in GROW model) 7, 42, 45, 55, 56, 58, 59, 61, 62, 63, 202, 208

Organization Culture and Quality of Service 165, 213, 215

P

Pareto Principle 127, 129

Paulus, Trina 207, 214

Personal investment opportunity 14, 21, 27, 32, 38, 46, 51, 57, 62, 69, 82, 88, 93, 99, 105, 111, 117, 124, 131, 146, 154, 161, 167, 173, 182, 187, 197, 203, 209

Pilsifer, Catherine 165

Plan See also *Action* 13, 14, 50, 64, 67, 68, 70, 80, 86, 92, 95, 97, 100, 166, 194, 213, 217

Player, Gary 44

Psycho-cybernetics 62, 213, 215

Q

Questioning 13, 29, 31, 33, 56, 57, 79, 81, 89, 91, 92, 93, 97, 109, 111, 123, 135, 136, 137, 144, 188, 194, 195, 208, 209

R

RAS See also Reticular activating system 45, 47, 49, 62, 63, 74, 202, 210

Renshaw, Ben 43, 213, 214, 215

Reticular activating system See also RAS 45, 47, 49, 62, 74, 79, 201

Robinson, Eddie 185, 214, 215

Rohn, Jim 11, 12, 103, 105, 214

Role model 77, 81

Rowling, J.K. 25, 27, 214

Russell, John 151, 214

S

School of Coaching, The 153

Schuck, Heather 143, 147, 214

Self-image 63, 121

Self-talk 119, 121, 122, 123, 124, 125, 181, 182

Seligman, Martin 116, 179, 180, 213, 215

Skill/will matrix model 109

SMART (goal-setting) 47, 50, 51

Socio-gram (social linking) 185, 187

Stage of Life 20, 21

Supercoaching 43, 213, 214, 215

T

Taxonomies of questioning 91

TGROW (GROW) 49

This Much I Know About Love Over Fear 167

Time for Coaching 159, 213, 214, 216

Tomsett, John 167, 168, 213, 216

V

Vale, Jason 67, 69, 214

Values in Action Signature Strengths Test See also *VIA* 116, 117

VIA See also *Values in Action Signature Strengths Test* 116, 117

W

Waitley, Denis 49, 50, 51, 214, 216

Ward, Barbara 85, 86, 87

Wheel of Life 23, 26, 27, 28, 31, 74

Whitmore, Sir John 109, 112, 143, 213, 214, 215

Will (in GROW model) 45, 67

Printed in Great Britain
by Amazon